BRAZIL

1989/1990 Edition

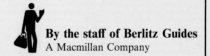

By the staff of Berlitz Guides
A Macmillan Company

**2nd Printing
1989/1990 Edition**

How to use our guide

- A background look at Brazil and its people is given in a general **introduction** starting on p. 9.
- Sightseeing **highlights** of each place visited can be found from p. 17 to p. 104.
- Practical **information** and helpful hints on planning your trip are given in alphabetical order from p. 117 to p. 124.
- **Eating ont** is covered by a comprehensive round-up of Brazil's culinary delights starting on p. 105, with a guide to selected **souvenir-buying** on pp. 113–116.
- And for quick reference, there is an **index** on pp. 125–128.

Although we make every effort to ensure the accuracy of all the information in this book, changes occur incessantly. We cannot therefore take responsibility for facts, prices, addresses and circumstances in general that are constantly subject to alteration. Our guides are updated on a regular basis as we reprint, and we are always grateful to readers who let us know of any errors, changes or serious omissions they come across.

General Editor: Nicholas Campbell
Layout: Doris Haldemann
Photos: pp. 2–3, 8, 15, 22, 25, 45, 83, 87, 89, 107, 108, 109, 111, 113, 114, 115, 117 Eric Jaquier; pp. 31, 35, 43, 49, 55 KEY-color/ZEFA; p. 12 KEY-color; cover, pp. 37, 65, 67, 71, 74, 75, 77, 81, 93, 97, 99 PRISMA/Schuster GmbH; p. 17 Pinheira, France; p. 53 Spectrum Colour Library; p. 59 Tony Stone Associates; p. 61 Image Bank/G. Guittard; p. 69 Danièle Luini.
We are grateful to Rilijeanne Castro-Campbell, Gabriel Barbosa, Maria Helena Grebot, John and Yvonne Kidner, Adrienne Jackson and Jonathan Sion for their help in preparing this guide. We also thank the Brazilian tourist organization Embratur and Varig Airlines for their co-operation.
Cartography: 🖋 Falk-Verlag, Hamburg

Contents

Getting Around

Our book follows the pattern of Brazil's natural regions—South-east, North-east, North, Centre-West and South—and traces a route that concentrates on the main cities and high-spots of any tour of the country. Because of the vast distances involved, it's almost impossible to cover everything comfortably in one go. Therefore, we've chosen an order of priorities aimed at suiting the average visitor with only limited time to explore.

We set off from the major departure point, Rio de Janeiro—exuberant tourist capital, with an unflagging zest for life and those legendary beaches that somehow never need describing. Then inland to São Paulo—economic driving-force of the country and the biggest city in Latin America. After that, Belo Horizonte, first city in Brazil to be conceived and built from scratch, and the "golden" city of Ouro Preto.

Through Vitória, part of it slumbering in a colonial dream, to the pulsating night life of Salvador. Recife, the Venice of Brazil, and Fortaleza complete the sparkling trio of north-eastern coastal resorts.

The atmosphere changes dramatically as we cross to the immense Amazon. A river journey touches the Amazonian wild life and often-elusive Indian tribes, giving portraits of Belém and Manaus—fascinating colonial relics that saw splendour then obscurity on the capricious wave of the jungle rubber boom.

Back to civilization ... with a vengeance! Brasília, futuristic capital and mirror of a country that always seems to bounce back from the doldrums. Curitiba, Smiling City of the South, precedes a trip to the mighty Iguaçu Falls and, to round off the tour, Porto Alegre—gateway to Gaucho country.

For any tour of Brazil, the emphasis has to be on air travel. Armed with a Brazil Air Pass, you can take full advantage of sophisticated air services that link even the most far-flung places. Trains, though relatively few and far between, offer a colourful close-up of landscape and life outside the cities—for example, the efficient sleeper service between Rio and São Paulo or the dramatic ride from Curitiba to Paranaguá.

Long-distance buses provide a comfortable solution if you want to travel stretches not covered by a concessionary air ticket. Car hire is another alternative. In the main, the roads are better in the south and south-east. If driving long distances, always check that you'll be able to get fuel on the way.

Brazil and the Brazilians

The flight from New York to Rio de Janeiro, which takes close to ten hours, covers a distance of more than 4,200 miles. By coincidence, that's nearly the length of Brazil's Atlantic coastline. There's an awful lot of beaches in Brazil.

Endless strands of blinding sands may be what lure you to South America's largest nation, and they'll never disappoint you. But spare the time to persevere beyond the beachhead, to the ranches and vineyards, lush plantations and steamy rain forest, sleepy colonial towns and skyscrapered cities tingling with life.

Staggeringly rich with promise, Brazil has often been called the land of the future. Cynics add that it always will be. In the 1980s many a big-time banker lost heart—and sleep—when Brazil entered the record books for running up the world's most burdensome international debt.

If the unstoppable flood of red ink conjures up visions of a country submerged by Third World hopelessness, be reassured. Brazil, resourceful and resilient, can feed itself. It also enjoys immense reserves of iron, bauxite and timber. It manufactures and exports transport planes and military vehicles. And the phones work.

The nation's most dependable—and endearing—source of wealth is its people, more than 135 million of them. This high-spirited, motley crowd comes in all colours and classes: miners, midwives and mystics, office workers and gun-toting politicians, football superstars and bathing beauties, cowboys and Indians. The cowboys—*gaúchos*—look after one of the world's largest herds of cattle; the small minority of pure-blooded Indians include tribesmen still cocooned in the Stone Age.

The racial melting pot in Brazil is as original and complex as the favourite, filling Saturday lunch, *feijoada*, with its all-embracing quota of meats, vegetables, spices and fruit. First there were the indigenous Indians, then the white colonists arrived from Portugal, then millions of African slaves, then the Asian immigrants. Stirred at length, the mixture produced people in every conceivable racial permutation.

Separated by great distances and varied backgrounds, the people of Brazil tend to defy generalizations. But three elements of their personality are evident everywhere: sense of honour, sense of humour, and sensuality. You can hardly miss the old-fashioned chivalry and the wry little jokes. And as for the fleshly appetites, a gauge might be the beauty, grace and unaffected sexiness of Brazil's young women. World-weary experts avow there is nothing like the sight of a graceful girl on Copacabana or Ipanema, bronzing her naturally *café-au-lait* complexion, her modesty covered with a thimbleful of *avant-garde* bathing suit. The eminent geographer Alberto Ribeiro Lamego was moved to write a paean to this voluptuous phenomenon: "The Universal Woman."

For the local men, the only other subject of overriding interest is soccer, whether watched in a stadium or played on the beach, in the street, or anywhere a game can be picked up. Football stars are the kings of democratic Brazil, and every slum lad hopes to kick his way to fame and fortune. The bigtime players enjoy all the rights and responsibilities of celebrity and once or twice in a lifetime a footballer like Pelé goes on to become a national monument. Football and show business may well be the only paths to conspicuous success for the 25 percent of the population classified as illiterate.

The dual preoccupations, sex and football, have produced the cult of the "body beautiful", male and female. On the beach, for instance, muscles and curves are cultivated as assiduously as greenhouse tomatoes in the Arctic. Jogging and working out were popular in Brazil long before the word "fitness" blustered into the international vocabulary.

What with all the workouts, and dancing into the night, Brazilians have little energy left for the belligerence that bristles in other climes. Anything but pushy, they tend to laugh off, rather than confront, an argument. And they've never been angry enough to stage a full-scale revolution.

A lot of fervour is devoted to religion. Brazil is often described as the country with more Catholics than any other, which may be statistically undeniable. But what's Catholic in Rio or Bahia might raise more than a few eyebrows in Rome. The Vati-

BRAZILIAN COAST

```
OCEANO
ATLÂNTICO

Baía de Marajó

BELÉM
        Baía de São José
    São Luís    Parnaíba
                    FORTALEZA
            Teresina
                        Natal
    Porto Franco      João Pessoa
                    RECIFE
            Petrolina
                        Maceió
    Barreiras    Xique-
                 Xique    Aracaju
                    SALVADOR
                Baía de Todos
                os Santos
BRASÍLIA
    Goiânia    Montes
               Claros
            BELO
            HORIZONTE
    Barretos        Vitória
        SÃO    Volta
        PAULO  Redonda
               RIO DE    Niterói
    Ourinhos   Santos JANEIRO
    Curitiba
      Paranaguá

      Florianópolis

PORTO ALEGRE

OCEANO ATLÂNTICO

                N

0        500 km

0        500 miles
```

can's teachings have been superimposed on the beliefs of Afro-Brazilian cults, known locally as Macumba, Candomblé or Xangô. Every Catholic saint has his pagan counterpart, so lighting a candle in church is not so different from burning one at a pagan ceremony.

Africa also underlies the most typical music of Brazil: the samba. The rhythm, which calls to mind native drums at their most evocative, compels participation: a tapping toe at the least, more likely a public spectacle. If you miss Carnival in Rio don't fret; something's always brewing—rehearsals for Carnival, or the celebration of some other holiday, screaming with colour and life.

While the rest of South America speaks Spanish, the language of Brazil is Portuguese—and don't you forget it! If all else fails, try a few words of Spanish, which Brazilians can decipher.

The linguistic and cultural split between Brazil and the rest of the continent was preordained even before Brazil was officially discovered. Under the Treaty of Tordesillas, in 1494, Portugal and Spain conspired to divide the New World between them. A vertical line was drawn down the still-hypothetical map of the western hemisphere. The Brazilian coast, east of the divide, was reserved, sight unseen,

Samba and smile symbolize the Brazilians' love of life.

for exploitation by Portugal. (Spaniards later suspected that Portugal must have secretly known all about Brazil.)

The actual discovery, in 1500, sounds like a bit of an anticlimax. What explorer Pedro Álvares Cabral took for an Atlantic island turned out to be the mainland of the

South American continent. Even so, he was not greatly impressed by the local populace, uncultivated tribesmen resembling the ones Columbus had misnamed Indians.

Economically, the place looked lacklustre. The only natural resource of commercial importance seemed to be a

Keystone-Press, Zürich

very tall tree named *pau-brasil* (brazil wood), valuable in Europe in the production of a reddish dye for textiles. Thus the country was named for the tree, and not the other way around.

Colonization began half-heartedly. Then Portugal noticed that the French were also trying to settle the coast, whereupon Lisbon hastily sent out further expeditions. These established new towns, and industry: Indians were enslaved to fell trees and plant sugar cane. As the sugar business sweetened, more labour was needed. Millions of additional slaves had to be imported from black Africa; they mixed with the white and Indian population, complicating the racial diversity of the colony.

Brazil revelled in a gold rush at the end of the 17th century, swiftly followed by the discovery of diamonds. To put the power closer to the wealth the capital was moved from Salvador da Bahia to Rio de Janeiro.

The 19th century news from Europe jolted Brazil. When Napoleon invaded Portugal, the Portuguese royal household escaped to Brazil and set up an interim capital in Rio. The distinctly provincial city on beautiful Guanabara Bay thus was destined to take on an unlikely imperial importance. Cutting itself adrift from the mother country, Brazil proclaimed itself an independent empire. It's been a republic since 1889, one year after the abolition of the slave trade. Since then, politicians and military juntas have alternated through the revolving door. In 1960 the door was moved to a brand new capital city, 80 minutes north-west of Rio by jet. The establishment of Brasília was a visionary plan to move the nation's centre of gravity, to open the immense interior wilderness.

Covering a greater area than the 48 mainland states of the U.S., Brazil borders on ten countries. In fact, it shares frontiers with all the nations of South America except Ecuador and Chile. The world's largest tropical country is wide enough to cover four time zones. The average temperature up the Amazon on the Equator can be bearable but for the humidity; down south it's quite temperate. Though eccentric rainfall dooms parts of the country to the threat of flood or drought, Brazil is spared the kind of sudden natural disasters afflicting other beautiful lands, such as volcanoes, earthquakes and typhoons.

All of Brazil's big cities sparkle, either with sophistication or charm, or just the sand of their beaches.

South America's most populous city, São Paulo, is the economic capital of Brazil. It's also surprisingly cosmopolitan; like New York, it was a haven for immigrants—Italians, Portuguese, Spaniards, and hundreds of thousands of Japanese. And it's still a hardworking, ambitious city in a country where hectic pursuits are more usually shunned.

So-called knowledgeable travellers usually say that you should have been to a place years ago, before it was "spoiled". But Rio de Janeiro, still Brazil's tourist capital if not the political hub, is as glamorous and hedonistic as ever. Rio boasts the world's largest football stadium and a 60,000-seat "Sambadrome", beyond which there's dancing in the streets.

Third biggest city is the prettily named Belo Horizonte, a well-placed model of late 19th-century town planning. It's the capital of Minas Gerais, the mineral state, also rich in picturesque old colonial towns.

With well over a million

inhabitants, Recife is the metropolis of the north-east. Its waterways and bridges inspired the slogan "the Venice of Brazil", but the sweeping beaches and African-style folklore make up for the shortage of gondolas.

The most lovable of the big north-eastern cities, Salvador, capital of Bahia state, has hundreds of churches and other precious colonial monuments, African-derived folklore and cuisine, and beaches galore.

Porto Alegre, another million-plus metropolis, offers a total change of pace: a modern, prosperous, riverside city set between southern Brazil's wine-producing and cattle-raising regions.

Porto Alegre and many other Brazilian cities grew because of the proximity of a river or the ocean. These provide some of the country's most truly spectacular attractions. The Atlantic, obviously, delivers unending scenic delight. But then there's the Amazon, more than two thousand miles long, which creates the character of half the national area; it contains the world's largest and thickest rain forest. Therein flourish thousands of species of plants, from towering trees to the most delicate orchids. Another watery advantage, economic as well as ornamental: Brazil's waterfalls, as nebulous as a plume of spray on the edge of the jungle, or as supreme as Iguaçu.

Even if it's always going to be the land of the future, now is a perfect time to see Brazil.

Macumba—standard medicine for the spirit or the soul.

Facts and Figures

Geography: South America's largest country, and the fifth largest in the world, Brazil covers nearly half the continent. The area, mostly tropical, is 3,286,470 square miles (8,511,957 sq. km.). To the north, Brazil borders French Guiana, Suriname, Guyana, Venezuela and Colombia; to the west, Peru and Bolivia; and to the south, Paraguay, Argentina and Uruguay. Its eastern frontier is the Atlantic Ocean, with a coastline of some 4,500 miles (7,400 kilometres). There are more than a thousand rivers; the Amazon is navigable all the way to Iquitos, Peru—some 2,000 miles (3,200 km.) upstream. Brazil has no Andes-class mountains but Pico da Neblina is 3,014 metres (9,889 ft.) high.

Population: About 135 million, largest population in South America. Whites and almost-whites are the majority in a society mixing European, Indian, African and Asian elements.

Capital: Brasília (pop. Federal District 1.2 million)

Major Cities: São Paulo (metropolitan area 13 million), Rio de Janeiro (metropolitan area 9.5 million); among other cities of more than 1 million: Belo Horizonte, Recife, Salvador, Porto Alegre.

Government: Federative republic composed of 23 states, 3 territories and federal district (headquarters of the elected president, bicameral legislature, and judiciary).

Economy: Brazil produces bauxite, chromium, iron and manganese; crops such as coffee, cocoa, sugar, soybeans and cotton; and steel, cars, machinery and textiles.

Religion: Roman Catholic, with overtones of African cults.

Language: Portuguese.

South-east

RIO DE JANEIRO

Introduction

The first view of Rio de Janeiro simply takes your breath away. The blue sweep of the bay dappled with islands and surrounded by green hills; blinding white beaches fringed with palms; towering Sugar Loaf Mountain standing like a giant rock sentinel at the entrance to the harbour. You were prepared for the wonders of Rio—the gaiety, the carnival atmosphere, the dazzling women—but not for the sheer beauty of this sight.

Stretched out along Guanabara Bay, washed by the South Atlantic, Rio is Brazil's cultural, commercial and financial centre. The population is over seven million and multiplying fast, and there is an air of prosperity in the modern office blocks and apartment buildings, chic residential quarters, spacious squares, parks and gardens. But there is also a bleaker side to the city. Perched on the steep hillsides, shantytowns or *favelas* provide inadequate shelter for two million people, sharing only the view with the penthouses of the millionaires below.

Rio is about as close to the equator as Havana, which means that winter is merely a formality. In July the average temperature dips to 69° Fahrenheit. This scarcely interferes with the outdoor way of life, which keeps the people moored to sidewalk café tables.

Thanks to the climate and "body beautiful" fixation of the Cariocas (as the inhabitants of this city like to call themselves), a great deal of time and energy is devoted to outdoor sports. Barefoot in the sand, teams of footballers run full tilt, each player dreaming that one day he will be another Pelé. Joggers find plenty of company on the mosaic beachside pavements. Surfers and windsurfers fly through the waves, while hang-glider pilots execute lazy turns high above the sands.

And then there is the carnival, Rio's annual explosion of music, colour and joy. The last fling before the austere Lenten season starts in earnest the Friday before Shrove Tuesday (Mardi Gras), and goes on for five days and nights nonstop. More than half a million people, all in costume, march, dance and sing in the organized parades through the streets.

You couldn't say that Rio de Janeiro is typical of Brazil, because it is impossible to generalize about a country so large and so diverse. With an area of 3½ million square miles (8½ million sq. km.), it is the largest country in South America, and one of the most populous in the world.

The original inhabitants were Indians, but in the 16th century the Portuguese colonized the country. They enslaved the Indians, set up sugar and spice plantations and established the Roman Catholic faith and Portuguese language and culture. When the sugar mills needed more manpower, black slaves were imported from Africa. A tradition of intermarriage started by the Portuguese has resulted in today's multiracial—but harmonious—society.

Most of the people live along the coast, where Brazil's largest cities have grown up around natural harbours. 600 miles (960 km.) inland is the modern city of Brasília, Brazil's political capital since 1960. Previously that honour was held by Rio de Janeiro for 125 years.

But, if Rio is no longer the capital of Brazil, it still holds its place in the heart of the people. This gay, crowded metropolis throbs with life and laughter. And everywhere there is music—even a youngster shaking a matchbox is enough to set the rhythm of the samba. The Cariocas themselves call it *A Cidade Maravilhosa*–the Marvellous City. They ought to know.

A Brief History

16th century   The coastal area around present-day Rio is charted early in the century. A Portuguese navigator mistakes Guanabara Bay for the mouth of a river, and names the site Rio de Janeiro (River of January). The French are the first to settle in the area, but Portuguese troops force them out in 1567.

17th–18th centuries   Sugar and immense mineral wealth—much of it shipped out through Rio—make Brazil an economically interesting proposition for the Portuguese. African slaves, imported to work the cane fields, mix with the white and Indian population. Brazil is elevated from the status of colony to vice-royalty, and in 1763 the capital is moved from Salvador to Rio.

19th century	In 1807, the Portuguese royal court, looking for a safe haven from Napoleon's armies, retreats to Rio. King João VI returns to Lisbon in 1821, handing over Brazil to his eldest son, Dom Pedro. Portugal officially grants independence to Brazil in 1825, and Dom Pedro is declared Pedro I, Emperor of Brazil. Rio becomes a prosperous, civilized city under Pedro II, who rules for nearly half a century, but growing anti-monarchist sentiment forces him to abdicate in 1889. A federal republic, the United States of Brazil, is proclaimed.
20th century	By 1907, Rio's population has reached 800,000. World War I proves a boon to the Brazilian economy, and the country also benefits from choosing the winning side. The Great Depression brings suffering and unrest, leading a military junta to install dictator Getúlio Vargas. Under the Vargas regime, Brazil joins the Allies in World War II. Though ousted after the war, he is elected president in 1950, but commits suicide in 1954 after losing support among the military. President Kubitschek moves the nation's capital from Rio to Brasília in 1960, but Rio nonetheless remains one of the country's most prosperous and lively cities.

Sightseeing

Rio's momentous **harbour** has an area of about 160 square miles—room enough for supertankers, warships, ferryboats, yachts and dozens of islands and islets. You'll want to head from here to the city's renowned beaches.

Copacabana is more beautiful today than when it first caught the world's imagination. Almost all buses have been diverted from Avenida Atlântica, and the beachside walkway—paved with black and white stones in the undulating Portuguese style—is wide enough for all the strollers, joggers, cyclists and sightseers. On the landward side of the broad avenue, sidewalk cafés at crucial intervals supply Cariocas with that essential *chopinho* (ice-cold draft beer).

The peninsula separating Copacabana beach from **Ipanema** beach ends in a rocky outcrop called Ponta do Arpoador. There is an ideal surfing beach on the west side of this narrow neck of land,

GREATER RIO

Arpoador beach. In the area, a hilly municipal park named **Praça Garota de Ipanema** (Girl from Ipanema Plaza) honours the song, and the girls, responsible for the area's fame. These girls, in their ingeniously designed minimal swimsuits, are the most eye-opening attraction of all.

Inland, along the streets of Ipanema are found the most chic boutiques in all of Rio. Fashion of all sorts is the big talking point. Ipanema also has many of Rio's favourite bars and restaurants, full of atmosphere and loyal perennial clients.

While in the area around Ipanema, you might want to visit Rio's **Jardim Botânico** (Botanical Gardens). In 1809 the *Palma Mater,* the mother of all the royal palm trees in Brazil, was planted here; the seeds had been imported—stolen, actually—from the Indian Ocean island now called Mauritius. Avenues of descen-

dant royal palms still tower over all the other inhabitants of this garden and forest.

Among other highlights: six lakes, including a pond in which enormous lilies float like platters with upturned edges; the orchid nursery; and a special hothouse for insectivorous plants.

Beyond the botanical gardens in Gávea, just before the Dois Irmãos tunnel, is the entrance to **Parque da Cidade** (City Park). Formerly the es-

tate of the Marquis of São Vicente, it was opened to the public in 1941. The former manor house has become the Museu da Cidade (City Historical Museum).

Returning to the beach area, **Praia Vermelha,** quite close to town, tends to fill up with sunbathers. But "Red Beach" is also starting point for trips up **Pão de Açúcar** (Sugar Loaf), the famous rock standing guard over the entrance to Guanabara Bay. From its summit 1,293 feet above sea level, you can read Rio like a map.

The only way to reach the top of Sugar Loaf is aboard a cable car which makes the journey in two stages. The trip begins at the Estação do Teleférico. The first stage of the aerial itinerary takes you to the top of Morro da Urca, somewhat more than half as high as Sugar Loaf. At this first station, which also has good panoramas over Rio, there's a big restaurant, as well as shops and a curious little museum of mechanized marionettes. The next car leaves for the Sugar Loaf summit.

It's a short bus ride from

The Sugar Loaf—one of the world's most fabulous sights.

RIO DE JANEIRO

Vermelha to **Flamengo,** the beach closest to the business district. This man-made beach forms part of the venturesome **Flamengo Park** project, which pushed Rio's front garden out into the harbour. In a colossal landfill programme completed in 1960, nearly 300 acres were reclaimed from the harbour. Brazil's master landscape architect, Roberto Burle Marx, transformed the new terrain into an admirable green belt between the sea and the city, with room enough for a superhighway, monuments, museums and all manner of leisure facilities.

Overlooking the park from a bluff is a church so appealing you may want to make a side-trip for a closer look: the **Igreja de N. Sa. da Glória do Outeiro** (Gloria Church on the Hill). The interior walls are decorated with classic blue-and-white Portuguese *azulejos* (decorative tiles).

Flamengo Park also contains several museums, including the city's **Modern Art Museum,** formerly excellent but now recovering from a catastrophic fire in 1978.

Adjacent to Flamengo Park are the gardens of the **Museu da República** (Museum of the Republic), currently closed for structural repairs. This regal palace served as the official residence of the presidents of Brazil from 1896 to 1954. Everything in this mid-19th-century residence—floors, ceilings, walls, mirrors, chandeliers, furniture—is sensationally well done, an opulent prize worth preserving.

Leaving the Flamengo Park area for the nearby commercial district, **Avenida Rio Branco,** the city's main street, is the place to find the most impressive banks, airline offices and neoclassic public buildings. The initial project, undertaken at the turn of the 20th century, was quite far-sighted; a perfectly straight road over a mile long with a row of brazilwood trees planted down the middle.

A few blocks south of Rio Branco, critics of architecture vehemently disagree about the new **Catedral Metropolitana,** also called Catedral Nova, rising like a volcano on the horizon south-west of the convent complex. The design of the reinforced concrete and glass structure has been described as a truncated cone or an Etruscan pyramid. The cornerstone was laid in 1964. The nave is longer than a football field; 20,000 standing worshippers can be accommodated. Gigantic stained-glass

windows of bold modern design, one for each quadrant, flood the interior with sunlight. A plaque at the main entrance commemorates the day Pope John Paul II preached at the cathedral: July 2, 1980.

Though remnants of colonial architecture are scattered throughout Rio, the greatest concentration of historic monuments centres on **Praça XV de Novembro** (November 15 Square). This was the city's

Colonial colour brightens Rio's 20th-century concrete.

main square long before it received its present name, commemorating the day in 1889 when the Brazilian republic was proclaimed.

With your back to the bay, the elegant three-story colonial building on your left is the **Palácio dos Vice-Reis,** the former residence of the Portuguese viceroys, completed in 1743.

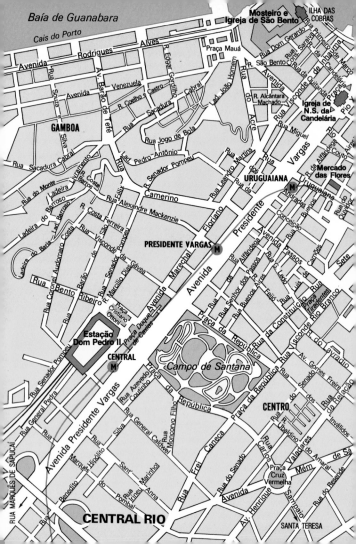

Across Rua 1° de Março from the square, two 18th-century churches are separated only by a narrow passageway. On the left, with a tall corner bell tower, is the **Igreja de Nossa Senhora do Carmo** (Carmelite Church), the former cathedral. In this Portuguese church, the emperor of Brazil was crowned.

The fine Baroque interior of the former cathedral is relatively modest compared with the **Igreja de N. Sa. do Monte do Carmo** (Church of Our Lady of Mount Carmel) right next door. Notice the exuberant decorations on the walls, the rich altar and the marble works of Mestre Valentim, the creator of the Praça XV fountain.

Avenida Vargas begins at Praça Pio X (Pius X Square), containing the cathedral-sized **Igreja de N. Sa. da Candelária.** Construction of this sumptuous church with Italianate features went on from about 1775 to 1810. The interior is entirely decorated with marble of remarkably varied colours: black, white, grey, yellow, green, red.

The **Igreja e Mosteiro de São Bento** (St. Bento Church and Monastery) provides a cool, quiet escape from the city's bustle. The church, part of a Benedictine monastery, was begun in 1633. Its simple but strong façade has twin towers capped with pyramids; large arched doorways with wrought-iron gates lead to 17th-century portals of finely carved wood. Inside, the florid decor reaches up to a painted, vaulted ceiling from which hang two heavy chandeliers.

The public entrance to the **Museu Histórico Nacional** (National Historical Museum) faces the main waterfront highway, near Praça XV de Novembro. The museum, established in 1922, took over one of the oldest buildings in Rio de Janeiro, the 16th-century Fortaleza de São Tiago (St. James Fortress). Its cellars had been used as dungeons for slaves; later the building served as a military prison, an arsenal and the headquarters of the Royal Military Academy. You don't have to be well versed in Brazilian history to appreciate the displays of ceremonial swords and helmets, thrones and palatial furnishings.

When you've finished touring Rio's historic centre, head west on Avenida Presidente Vargas for **Maracanã.** The biggest soccer stadium in the world—capacity between 170,000 and 200,000 depending on how tightly the standing spectators can be squeezed in—is a sight to see even when it's empty.

Even if you're not a soccer fan, you'll be impressed by the size of the place. With all its complex facilities, Maracanã was rushed to completion in less than two years for the World Cup of 1950 (Brazil lost to Uruguay).

Near the Stadium, Brazil's **Museu Nacional** (National Museum), one of the oldest scientific institutions in Latin America, was founded in 1818 by King João VI. The three-story palace it now occupies was the residence of the royal family for 81 years. Specializing in anthropology and the natural sciences, the star exhibit is a meteorite which came to earth in the state of Bahia in 1888, weighing more than five tons. The museum grounds, called the **Quinta da Boa Vista,** actually make up the largest park in Rio, with a lake for pedal-boats and paddling and the city's **Jardim Zoológico** (zoo).

Also in the stadium area, the **Museu do Índio** (Indian Museum) features appealing ceramics in unusual colours, head-dresses of all ranks, dolls and musical instruments.

A short drive south brings you to the **Parque Nacional da Tijuca** (Tijuca National Park). Here, within the confines of a great metropolis, is all the jungle you'll ever want to see—and some breezy heights for relief from the heat.

In the early colonial development of Rio de Janeiro, the thick forests of the Tijuca mountainsides were felled for lumber and firewood. The land was then used for orchards and coffee plantations. A reforestation programme was undertaken in the middle of the 19th century, when Cariocas realized that the wilderness of Tijuca was worth saving.

The park has waterfalls, caves, and several impressive lookouts, including **Corcovado.** At 2,326 feet, Corcovado, meaning Humpbacked Mountain, is nearly twice as high as Sugar Loaf. In modern times it has become equally symbolic of the city of Rio de Janeiro. The statue of **Cristo Redentor** (Christ the Redeemer), with arms outstretched over the bay, was inaugurated as a national monument in 1931. The reinforced concrete statue, designed by the French sculptor Paul Landowski, is 98 feet tall; a small chapel is built into the base of the monument.

Petrópolis

Petrópolis is about 40 miles (65 km.) from the centre of Rio de Janeiro. Emperor Pedro II, after whom Petrópolis is named, established his summer capital here, among the relatively cool hills of the Serra dos Órgãos (Organ Mountains).

The scenery along the drive from Rio is a wonder of tropical colour: hortensia, hibiscus, bougainvillea, orchids. It is no great surprise to find banana sellers lying in wait along the road; the jungle here is full of banana plants, along with more exotic fruit trees and wild flowers.

The altitude of Petrópolis is officially 2,750 feet, which all but guarantees a measure of relief from the sea-level heat. But it's hardly the climate to justify the German- and Swiss-style chalets of the area. In part they're a fantasy, but they also recall the homesickness of the early colonists, mostly German.

By the second half of the 19th century, all of Rio society wanted to own a villa in Petrópolis, or at least spend the season in one of the town's luxurious hotels. The richly landscaped houses they built —in architectural styles as unlikely as Norman, Roman and Californian—are among the nicest relics of that golden age.

Whatever you plan to visit in Petrópolis, don't miss the **Museu Imperial.** The museum, inaugurated in 1945, is housed in the neoclassic Summer Palace, built exactly one century earlier.

Noteworthy paintings, tapestries and furniture fill the building, and the floors are so fine that visitors are required to don soft overshoes. The most valuable single exhibit, kept under armed guard, is the imperial crown of Pedro II. Its 639 diamonds, 77 pearls and gold construction add up to a weight of over 3 pounds. Other paraphernalia of power on view include the throne and sword of the emperor, as well as the regalia of the Order of the Garter conferred on him by Queen Victoria. You can also inspect his office as it was when he was deposed in 1889.

The **cathedral** of Petrópolis looks like a historic building, but it's a case of late 19th-century architects looking back with admiration on French Gothic churches. The building wasn't finished until 1939. Behind a wrought-iron fence are the tombs of Emperor Pedro II and the royal family.

South-east

SÃO PAULO

Introduction

Straight up, from the loftiest palm trees to the tops of the soaring skyscrapers, São Paulo is a city like New York gone mad—concrete, glass, super-highways and smog, with jungle sprouting all over it. Nobody quite knows where downtown is; one district runs into another, residential areas one block, business towers the next. Were the two simple priests, who arrived here with their cross and Bible in 1554, able to see this gigantic megapolis, it's difficult to say whether they'd be pleased or sorry. But they'd certainly be surprised.

This unique city of 10 million souls—and growing at a rate of a thousand a day—is the biggest industrial and commercial centre in Brazil. The greater São Paulo urban area is ten times the size of New York City. The huge buildings buzz with telephones, telexes and—talk. Businessmen fresh off the breakfast shuttle from Rio speed to their offices over a complex network of express-ways.

And yet, despite the sophistication, a frontier spirit lingers on in this largest of all Latin American cities. Because once fortunes had been made—in gold, diamonds, rubber, live-stock, coffee—the money had to be spent somewhere. The riches were ploughed back into the city. Gigantic structures—cork-screws, waves, towers, turrets and pyramids—testify to the creative spirit of Brazil's architects and engineers.

And that's not all: parks and museums, cool havens of rest and culture, dot the city, and São Paulo's myriad restaurants provide top cuisine from all over the world. As the sun goes down and the first lights of evening twinkle through the mist, tourists may begin to feel the spirit of the samba and sense why the city is some-times called "the business-man's heaven".

A Brief History

16th century   Pedro Álvares Cabral, a Portuguese explorer, dis-covers Brazil in 1500. Jesuit priests, Father José de Anchieta and Father Manuel da Nóbrega, set up a mission station and school on the Piratininga plateau (now central São Paulo) in1554.

17th–18th centuries	The cultivation of sugar cane and the discovery of gold and diamonds attract pioneer explorers and exploiters. The *bandeirantes,* using São Paulo as base, work their way inland. The coffee plant (from Guyana) is introduced and takes root in São Paulo's fertile *terra roxa* (red earth).
19th century	Business booms—so does immigration. Fortunes are made. Through the political changes of the century—independence in 1822 and proclamation of a republic in 1889—São Paulo retains the status of a growing economic centre.
20th century	New waves of immigrants—Poles, Italians, Germans and Japanese—arrive. Intensive cultivation continues; commerce and trade thrive. The great building boom begins, coupled with an increase in immigration, and following War II, São Paulo continues to grow faster than any other Latin American city. Projections predict a population of 20,000,000 for the year 2000.

Sightseeing

Seventy kilometres (40 mi.) from the sea, on a fertile plateau 700 metres (about 2,300 ft.) above sea level, São Paulo is somewhat cooler than Rio. Choose light, comfortable clothes to wear, and carry a sweater for the sudden drops of temperature—a standby you won't regret.

The general rule for those who want to drive themselves in São Paulo is, don't—unless you look on driving as a sport. Conditions are chaotic; traffic patterns are difficult to understand and nerves will not be soothed by joining in the roaring cacophony of honking autos. The best way to see the town is on foot (stash your wallet out of reach of pickpockets), with recourse to taxi, *metrô* (subway) or bus—in that order—where necessary. Below are listed São Paulo's "musts" —all more or less in the central area. With more time, you can take excursions to various points of interest in São Paulo state.

As good a place to start as any, the **Praça da Sé** (Cathedral Square) in the heart of the city, covers a vast *metrô* station. A million *Paulistanos* throng through the giant concourse daily. Fountains, landscaping, greenery and eye-catching sculpture fill the area.

The monumental **cathedral** *(Sé)* was finally completed in 1970. The grandiose interior has room for 8,000 worshippers. São Paulo's very first chapel was also erected near this site (1554). Just north of the cathedral, the reconstructed **Capela de Anchieta** on the Pátio do Colégio stands as a tribute to the city's founding fathers.

From the Praça da Sé—to get into the swing of the city—take the Rua Direita, leading via the Praça do Patriarca to the **Viaduto do Chá** (Tea Viaduct). Seeing it, you may well need a cup of tea, if not something stronger. If you were to choose one single sight as best representative of São Paulo's overpowering reality, this would be it. Cars, buses, taxicabs and trucks—honking, humming, squealing and roaring—stream down 20 lanes under and over the huge viaduct—like electronic bips in a computer game. The area teems with life. If everywhere is "centre" in São Paulo, this is the centre of everywhere.

Ten minutes walk in any direction from Viaduto do Chá will provide the same scenery: towering buildings such as the wave-like **residential block** designed by the celebrated Brazilian architect Oscar Niemeyer in 1953 or the landmark **Edificio Itália** on the Avenida Ipiranga.

For all this impressive architecture, don't forget to watch out for the tiny churches *(igreja)* dotted about the area. Squeezed in between the mammoth towers, the churches of São Paulo will provide a moment of peace—for free. Some date back to the 16th century.

Hop in a cab for a change of scene and pace at the **Museu de Arte de São Paulo** on fashionable Avenida Paulista. This is, without doubt, the finest museum in São Paulo. The building was opened by Queen Elizabeth of Great Britain in 1968. Delicate yet strong-looking, set atop slender pylons, the structure seems to defy gravity. Inside, the remarkable collection of Assis Chateaubriand fills the galleries with some great treasures of 14th- to 20th-century European painting. Contemporary Brazilian art works can also be seen.

Another important museum not to be missed, the **Museu de Arte Sacra** (Sacred Art Museum) near Tiradentes metro station, has a priceless collection of sacred art from all over the country. The museum is located in an ancient monas-

tery. Even a short visit will be an enriching experience.

Green grass, blue lakes, leafy trees and flowers of every hue account for the appeal of the vast and welcome **Ibirapuera Park** (*metrô* Ana Rosa). The main entrance is graced by the colossal **Monumento das Bandeiras.** This powerful work commemorates Brazil's pioneers, the men and women who set out to tame the primeval jungle in the 17th and 18th centuries.

It's all go on São Paulo's switchback highways.

There are several important museums and exhibition halls in Ibirapuera Park. Of particular interest are the **Museu de Arte Contemporânea** (Contemporary Arts Museum) and the **Museu de Arte Moderna** (Modern Art Museum).

São Paulo rounded off? Not quite. Don't miss an outing to one of São Paulo's most popular attractions: the **Instituto Butantã**, in the city's western sector. This is home to thousands of snakes, poisonous spiders and edgy-looking, live scorpions. Between the expressions of the unblinking reptiles and their horrified visitors it's hard to know who's outstaring whom, as expert keepers "milk" the serpents for the venom.

Other Excursions

You can conjure up one of the most emotion-charged moments in Brazilian history at São Paulo's **Parque da Independência** (Independence Park), in Ipiranga. It was here, on a memorable day in 1822, that the future Emperor Dom Pedro I drew his sword from its scabbard with the now-legendary Cry of Ipiranga (Grito do Ipiranga): "Independence or Death!" The small hut in the park where Dom Pedro stayed, the **Casa do Grito**, takes on a special significance for São Paulo each year on September 7—Brazil's National Day.

The declaration—immortalized in the national anthem —is marked in fitting style by the Ipiranga Monument. The body of the first emperor, together with his wife, Empress Leopoldina, lies in the **Capela Imperial** (Imperial Chapel) underneath.

While in the park, you can piece together aspects of São Paulo's colonial past at the **Museu Paulista**. Its collection includes maps, coins, period furniture, art works and a pictorial commentary on Indian culture.

The **Zoo** (metrô Jagueribe) and nearby **Jardim Botânico** (Botanical Gardens), about 40 minutes south of town, are specially good for visitors with children.

Even further out, **Embu**, 30 kilometres (20 mi.) from central São Paulo is an animated and delightful arts and crafts mecca. On Sundays, artisans, local characters and traders from nearby villages gather to sell their colourful wares.

Finally **Santos**, São Paulo's huge port, sprawls along the Atlantic coast and the river estuary. Vast quantities of Brazilian produce fill the voluminous warehouses.

Along the sea front from here, you can catch a ferry to Guarujá, whose beaches attract crowds of Paulistanos —especially at the weekends. Watch the currents, though. Resort activities range from the most exhilarating of water sports to a leisurely round of golf.

South-east

BELO HORIZONTE
OURO PRETO

Introduction

Booming, boisterous, larger than life—Belo Horizonte was born to be state capital. It was no mere coincidence that the city blossomed so conveniently on a plateau poised centrally enough to take over the administration and economy of Minas Gerais. No, it was a carefully planned birth.

The state authorities had long since wanted to transfer the capital from Ouro Preto, an undisputed 18th-century treasure of a city but hardly geared to the needs of progressive politics. Since there were no suitable contenders for the title, one was created. And with this kind of strategic planning, it isn't surprising that the chessboard concept of Belo Horizonte emerged. Streets were laid out uniformly, with a second chessboard of avenues at a 45-degree angle to the first.

Four years later, in 1897, a site already graced with the name Beautiful Horizon had a city worthy of it, cushioned by the great mountains of the Serra do Espinhaço.

Belo Horizonte—Brazil's first city to be "planted" en bloc—grew from small beginnings. In 1900, three years after its inauguration, there were 13,500 townspeople. By 1960, the population numbered almost 7,000, and today—less than 100 years since it was created—the city is teeming with more than two million *Mineiros* from all over the state.

Mind you, you could be forgiven for failing to recognize the model of Belo Horizonte's planning—Washington, DC—in the sprawl of industrial development that went hand-in-hand with the population explosion.

At a height of 850 metres (2,789 feet), the endless plain is relieved by the white stone skyscraper blocks and, beyond, the smoky silhouettes of the *serra*. Some days even the mountains fade into a more distant relief against the skyscrapers. It's an impressive sight.

From far out, the hills take on a rusty hue that characterizes one of the country's richest mining and mineral areas. Nearby Nova Lima claims the deepest iron ore mine in the world, and Belo Horizonte has a major steelworks.

These days, gold is much less in evidence, but there are treasures of another kind: Ouro Preto has retained its architectural charm and is a delight to visit. Once a year, it becomes state capital again for a day—a fitting symbolic gesture to this model of baroque splendour. Other notable towns include São João del Rei, Congonhas do Campo, Mariana, Tiradentes and Diamantina, birthplace of former Brazilian President Juscelino Kubitschek.

And the *Mineiros?* They may sometimes be considered rather slower in thought and action than other Brazilians, but they have a reputation for reliableness and efficiency. Some would compare themselves to the Swiss, pointing to the abundance of banks, cows and cheese. There the comparison ends...if only because an average temperature of 20 °C (68 °F) doesn't allow for much snow.

A Brief History

17th century   Expeditions *(bandeiras)* forge a way inland, exploring what will become Minas Gerais state. Soon after the discovery of gold there in the 1690s, the first settlement is founded by the leader of a group of *bandeirantes*, Antônio Dias de Oliveira. The population grows, the area develops economically and Portugal imposes taxes on the settlers.

18th century   Dias de Oliveira's settlement is formally elevated to the status of town *(vila)* in 1711. The following year it is named Vila Rica (Rich Town) because of the gold finds. An insurrection against Portuguese rule, the Revolta Filipe dos Santos, breaks out in 1720. Following a siege of the town, the revolt is put down. An independence movement later takes root in Vila Rica. It is supressed in 1789 and the leader, Joaquim José da Silva Xavier (Tiradentes), is executed.

19th century   In 1823, Vila Rica is given city status and becomes capital of the province of Minas Gerais. It is renamed Ouro Preto (Black Gold). Following the proclamation of a republic in 1889, Minas Gerais becomes a state. Eight years later, the capital is changed from Ouro Preto to Cidade de Minas—the first city to be completely planned and built in the Brazilian interior.

BELO HORIZONTE

20th century   In 1901, Cidade de Minas is given a new name, Belo Horizonte (Beautiful Horizon). Ouro Preto is declared a national monument in 1933. During the 1940s, Mayor Juscelino Kubitschek of Belo Horizonte creates an industrial centre in the Contagem district and a large park, with the futuristic structures of architect Oscar Niemeyer, in the district of Pampulha. Kubitschek becomes President of Brazil in 1956 for four years. In 1980, the United Nations Educational, Scientific and Cultural Organization—UNESCO—declares Ouro Preto a cultural monument for all mankind.

Sightseeing

A pleasant spot to begin a tour is the **Municipal Park** (Parque Municipal), in the heart of downtown Belo Horizonte, the city's administrative and financial centre. The park itself has an enormous diversity of trees and pretty ornamental gardens with ponds. There, too, is the **Palácio das Artes,** where traditional handcrafted souvenirs are on view in the Centro de Artesanato Mineiro. For children, a relaxing interlude is provided by the park's playground and amusements.

Not far from here, in the impressively palm-lined Praça da Liberdade (Liberty Square), is the Governor's residence, the **Palácio da Liberdade.** That, together with the other neighbouring buildings, carries an enchanting air of *belle époque.* Belo Horizonte's **History Museum** (Museu Histórico) brings to life again the atmosphere of the original settlement, Arraial do Curral del Rei, with fascinating exhibits displayed in a *fazenda* (ranch house) building.

In contrast, the **Praça da Assembléia** is lined with modern buildings, including the state parliament (Assembléia Legislativa) and the Banco do Brasil. The city's varied selection of museums includes the Museu da Cidade (City Museum), the Museu Mineiro, the Mineralogy Museum, the Museu do Telefone and the Museu de História Natural (Natural History Museum).

South of downtown, on the Serra do Curral, is the **Parque das Mangabeiras,** a wooded park with amenities and space for picnics. A monument marks the spot where Pope

John Paul II gave an address.

Fine examples of the work of Brazilian architect Oscar Niemeyer—who designed much of the national capital, Brasília—can be seen in **Pampulha,** a startlingly modern suburb 8 kilometres (5 mi.) from the city centre. The Museu de Arte Moderna (Museum of Modern Art) stands in glass-and-marble splendour, originally a casino until gambling was banned after the last war. Pampulha's ultra-modern chapel, the Capela de São Francisco de Assis, rises in hangar style, the main outer wall sweeping up diagonally and back down at a 60-degree angle in an unbroken line. Take time to study the undulating exterior at the back of the building and the murals inside by Brazilian painter Cândido Portinari.

The vast bowl-shaped stadium in Pampulha, the **Estádio Governador Magalhães Pinto**—known as the Mineirão—is the second-biggest in the world after the Maracanã stadium in Rio. It seats comfortably 110,000 spectators, which—even for Brazil—is some football crowd. At the end of the giant man-made lake is the **Jardim Zoológico** (Zoo), not far from Pampulha Airport.

Ouro Preto

The red-tiled roofs of Ouro Preto are laid out carefully across the hillsides, interlocking like an unfinished jigsaw puzzle with clumps of foliage sprouting through to fill up the gaps. Either side of the quaintly cobbled streets, the little houses lean into one another as they thread their way up and over steep slopes past the delicately sculpted façades of churches, chapels and mansions.

The Genius of Aleijadinho

Ouro Preto's most gifted sculptor, Antônio Francisco Lisboa, had to cope with a crippling handicap. Afflicted by leprosy when he was young, his limbs became deformed and he lost completely the use of his hands.

Undeterred, Lisboa had tools tied to his arms and worked on despite the debilitating disease, carving religious masterpieces with sensitivity and feeling. He already had one social disadvantage, having been born the mulatto son of a Portuguese architect and an African slave.

Seeing his hunched body at work day after day, the people of Ouro Preto nicknamed him Aleijadinho—Little Cripple. It was to become one of the most respected names in baroque architecture.

This perfect example of a baroque city frozen in time was once, rather prematurely, called the "rich town"—prematurely, since it was 14 years before the gold that had drawn settlers here could be used to construct a place able to live up to the description. Later, it became Ouro Preto—"Black Gold", after the fine, dark grains of the precious metal panned in the Rio Tripuí, the river that runs through the valley.

Fronting on to the main square, Praça Tiradentes, is the former **Governors' Palace** (Palácio dos Governadores), built in 1742. The building contains the School of Mines (Escola de Minas)—established in 1876—which still serves as a school of mining and mineralogy. Its museum is said to be one of the best in the world, boasting an extensive collection of gems, black gold, crystal and stones containing gold.

Opposite stands the **Museu da Inconfidência,** a museum of art and history which has drawings by the famous baroque sculptor Aleijadinho. The building, dating from last century, has also served as a prison. Next to it is **Carmo Church** (Igreja de Nossa Senhora do Carmo), the façade of which is Aleijadinho's work. Much of his acclaimed statuary can also be seen in the **Church of St. Francis of Assisi** (Igreja de São Francisco de Assis), in addition to paintings by Mestre Ataíde, a contemporary of his.

Aleijadinho's tomb is in **Antônio Dias Church,** together

with a museum illustrating his aesthetic accomplishments. His father's earlier talent is illustrated in the **Igreja do Pilar** (Pilar Church).

Appropriately enough, a statue of freedom fighter Tiradentes stands today in **Praça da Independência.** His home was in Rua São José, now part of the commercial district. On the site of the Tiradentes home is the Association commerciale building. You'll be able to picture the conspiratorial atmosphere at the meeting place

Ouro Preto—a rich setting for the city built by gold.

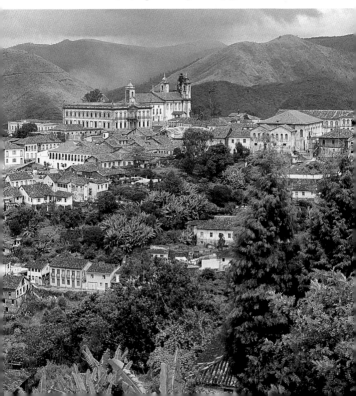

of the revolutionaries, the **Casa de Reunião dos Inconfidentes.**

Also worth seeing is the **Casa dos Contos,** once the state treasury and now converted into a museum. Its archives show impressive examples of civilian architecture in colonial times.

Holy Week processions that draw thousands are held in Ouro Preto. One of the most moving is the Good Friday procession that celebrates Christ's removal from the cross, and on the Sunday a mile-long carpet of flowers stretches from Pilar Church to Antônio Dias Church as part of the Resurrection celebration.

The Tooth-Puller's Revolution

Some two hundred years ago, Ouro Preto was a hotbed of revolution. Based there was an independence movement, the Inconfidência Mineira, led by a low-ranking army officer, Joaquim José da Silva Xavier—otherwise known as Tiradentes (Tooth-Puller) owing to his skill with the pincers.

The *inconfidentes* (conspirators) were discontented with the actions of the Portuguese Queen, Maria I, whom they accused of stifling development in Brazil while at the same time relieving the country of all its gold. Not only that, they argued, but heavy taxes were being imposed to finance European high living.

Ideas of freedom that were to prompt the French Revolution later that year, 1789, also inspired Tiradentes. His revolt against Portuguese domination was timed to coincide with increased taxes.

Unfortunately for the *inconfidentes,* somebody betrayed them to the Minas Gerais governor.

Queen Maria was not in a forgiving mood. After being locked in a tiny cage for three years, Tiradentes was hanged and quartered. His body was ceremoniously disposed of, his house demolished and salt spread over the land so that nothing could grow there again. The other *inconfidentes* were more fortunate. After a while, their death sentences were commuted and they were deported.

Tiradentes was to remain the symbol of freedom for Brazil. In 1822, exactly 30 years after his execution, his dream was realized—Dom Pedro I declared independence. And the rallying-cry of the *inconfidentes* lives on in the Minas Gerais flag and coat-of-arms: "Liberty, even if it comes late..."

South-east

VITÓRIA

Introduction

Like many other towns and cities of Brazil, Vitoria owes its development to the discovery of gold. When the precious metal came to light in the neighbouring state of Minas Gerais at the end of the 17th century, it was sent officially to Rio de Janeiro for exportation by the Portuguese government. However, smugglers created their own routes through the dense forests and mountains to the small fishing villages along the eastern coast. The sleepy neighbouring settlements of Vitoria and Vila Velha, favourably positioned around a small harbour, became popular smuggling ports. They were eventually transformed into a fortified camp which became the administrative capital of the state of Espírito Santo two centuries later.

The small state, squeezed in between mountains and the sea, derives its income from the exportation of iron ore, timber and coffee. The long coastline is a profusion of unspoiled, sheltered beaches; the climate pleasant and less humid than that of Rio.

Vitoria was long isolated from the larger Brazilian cities and slumbered through the frenzied industrial expansion associated with much of Brazil. The city grew at a leisurely pace; much of its colonial charm has been retained. The inhabitants, known as *Capixabas* after a local Indian tribe, are easy-going and friendly.

A Brief History

16th century Portuguese navigators chart the coast north of the settlement of Rio de Janeiro. Towns and villages are built in secluded harbours along the coast; Vitoria and Vila Velha are constructed in 1551.

17th century Portuguese settlers flee from Dutch occupiers of the northern provinces of Brazil and many settle in the Vitoria region. Sugar plantations thrive. Gold is discovered in 1698 in the adjacent state of Minas Gerais.

18th century Diamonds are discovered in Minas Gerais in 1729. As sugar plantations decline, gold and diamond mines boom, inducing massive immigration from Rio. Smuggling is widespread. Vasco Fernando Coutinho is sent by the King of Portugal to overcome the smugglers, to defeat the pirates who plagued the coastal shipping lanes, and to combat hostile Indians. Vitoria is heavily fortified. Jesuit priests pacify many of the Indian tribes.

19th century	Vitoria becomes a wealthy capital and important exportation port. At the end of the century, Italian, Swiss and German immigrants settle in the mountains and establish small farms.
20th century	Agriculture expands, but massive industrialization bypasses Vitoria. Road and rail links connect Minas Gerais with Vitoria's export shipping terminals.

Sightseeing

Vitoria is built on an island, joined to the mainland by two bridges. The streets are neat and attractive, full of boutiques, fashionable shops and numerous outdoor cafés. Take a ride through the residential sector where colonial villas overgrown with bougainvillea and jacaranda share spectacular views of the beautiful harbour and coast.

A short stroll in from the harbour is the **cathedral,** decorated with ornate Portuguese tiles. It contains a magnificent golden altar in classic Baroque style.

A drive over either of Vitoria's bridges will bring you to **Vila Velha** (the Old Town), once the nucleus of the settlement. Overlooking the harbour is the ancient fortified monastery **Nossa Senhora da Penha** (Our Lady of the Rock). Work began in 1558 but most of the construction dates from the 17th and 18th centuries. It is now in ruins, but the climb is well worth it just for the superb views of Vitoria from the top of the hill.

The white-sand beaches at Vila Velha and Praia da Costa are among the most beautiful in the whole country. Further south, **Guarapari** boasts a unique, black beach of radioactive monazitic sands, renowned for therapeutic cures of rheumatism, neuritis and other complaints.

Two inland villages merit a visit: Santa Leopoldina and Domingos Martins, both situated about 28 miles from Vitoria. They preserve the architecture and customs of the German and Swiss immigrants who arrived in the 18th century. Santa Leopoldina has a museum with an interesting display covering the early years of settlement.

Further Afield

Towards the western border of the state, the splendid Caparaó National Park contains one of Brazil's highest mountains, the 2,890–metre (9,482–ft) **Pico da Bandeira.** The Belo Horizonte road runs quite close, and you can get from there to within a few miles of the mountain, as far as the village of Ibitirama. If you're super-fit, a good guide and a couple of days are all you need to get to the top and back; otherwise, you can find plenty of interesting walks in the National Park.

Heading north, you can discover numerous places to sunbathe and look out on the sunkissed waters of the Atlantic.

A diverting ride through picturesque countryside takes you to the hill-town of **Santa Teresa,** near the Nova Lombardia National Biological Reserve. If you would like a chance to look round the hummingbird sanctuary there, check in advance—otherwise, the two-hour journey would still be worth taking.

Closer still to Salvador, you encounter the dazzling beaches of **Conceição da Barra,** deservedly rated among the best along this part of the coast.

Land Ahoy!

On April 22, 1500, on board a fleet of ships sailing west across the Atlantic, the cry went up: *"Terra à vista!"* ("Land ahoy!"). It was the east coast of Brazil—the first land to be seen in a long and stormy voyage from Portugal.

The Portuguese, under navigator Pedro Álvares Cabral, went ashore. Finding it a calm spot, they called it Porto Seguro (safe port). And, as it was Easter, they named the mountain that had first been sighted Monte Pascoal (Easter Mount).

Another geographical assumption wasn't quite so accurate. They called the area Ilha de Vera Cruz, thinking they had landed on an island. Later, realizing the error, Cabral corrected the name to Terra de Santa Cruz.

Somehow, though, the name didn't seem to stick, and eventually the word Brasil emerged—deriving from the trees of pau-brasil (brazil wood) that were of such interest in Europe because of their red pigmentation that could be used to dye materials simply and effectively.

Grateful for their safe landing, the Portuguese fleet's priest, Frei Henrique de Coimbra, celebrated a mass—the first in Brazil. A cross still marks the spot.

North-east

SALVADOR

Introduction

All Saint's Day, November 1st, 1501: a small ship bears down the coast of an unknown continent. At her helm is the Italian adventurer Amerigo Vespucci, skippering under the Portuguese flag. Suddenly land is sighted. On the horizon a line of sandy beach curves into the distance as far as the eye can see. With thanksgiving and prayers, the tiny vessel heaves to on the site of São Salvador da Bahia de Todos os Santos (Holy Saviour of the Bay of All Saints)—Bahia state capital.

Salvador has no equal on earth. Colonial mansions and Baroque churches decorated with ornate gold leaf coexist with holiday hotels, shanty-town huts and elegant restaurants. And surrounding the peninsula on which the city stands is mile upon mile of hot empty beach with room for just about everybody in Brazil. Here you don't have to wait your turn to dive into the Atlantic. Everyone could jump in at once.

Religion is a way of life in Salvador. Roman Catholic Masses are said alongside *candomblé* rituals, Christian saints are mixed up with African gods, and everything in an atmosphere of carnival, samba and *futebol* (football)—South America's favourite sport. Rhythmic strains are everywhere, so are smiling faces—brown, black, white but never blue. In Salvador a Monday morning feeling is virtually unknown.

But even if one of Salvador's graciously dressed ladies in fresh white lace and colourful batik gown should lose her poise, there would always be a way to recover it quickly. A seafood snack, a bright new golden bangle, a song in the sunshine or today's saint's feast day. One of those will surely put things right.

For the visitor, it's a fascinating place. There are old forts and ancient churches, colourful gardens and lively markets. Museums and art galleries add to the attractions, providing a record of Salvador's past from the sugar era to the recent building boom. The city is the home of *capoeira* entertainments, the traditional slave dancing in which agile acrobats sail through the air to the rhythm of drums—beating out a story from another age.

As all of today's cities, Salvador hasn't quite been able to keep modern problems out. The rise in population added to pockets of poverty in the city's outlying districts has meant an increase in petty crime. After twilight hours, you may be solicited. A polite but firm "no" is usually enough to get free.

Bewitched, bewildered, or just plain delighted—whatever you think of Salvador, it won't be indifference. Take a notebook to jot down your experiences for, as the old saying goes: The palest ink is stronger than the best memory. And you won't want to forget Salvador.

A Brief History

16th century	Explorer Amerigo Vespucci discovers the bay in 1501. Military Governor Tomé de Souza, on instructions from King João III, establishes Salvador as capital of Brazil in 1549. Slaves from West Africa are imported to work the land.
17th century	Great decades of Baroque construction begin. The Dutch attack Salvador but are repulsed. Forts are built and garrisons strengthened.
18th–19th centuries	Interest shifts from sugar and cocoa industries as gold and other minerals are discovered in the Minas Gerais region. Salvador loses the title of capital to Rio in 1763. Slaves revolt, but are brutally suppressed in 1825. For the next 100 years Salvador stays a backwater.
20th century	Industrialization, the development of the petrochemical industry and, especially of late, tourism become primary sources of income. City administrators pledge to preserve Salvador's unique cultural heritage.

Sightseeing

In Salvador if you ask a passer-by to direct you downtown, don't be surprised if he tells you to take the elevator. Because half the city really is down. The lower town (cidade baixa) sprawls out along the waterfront at the bottom of a 200-foot (70-metre) cliff—on which the rest of the city (cidade alta) is built.

A good place to start your visit is at the **lookout point** near the Lacerda elevator. From here you'll be rewarded with a panoramic view of the lower town and the fabulous **bay** (Baia de Todos os Santos).

Daring to challenge the serene blue of the majestic bay, perkily coloured boats and still green islets are scattered like charms over the water.

In the foreground, just offshore, the powerful-looking **Forte de São Marcelo** (1623) protects the port. With walls a metre thick, the fort was designed to withstand the most determined marauding pirate. From the lookout point you can also see the customs house and market place—overcrowded with bustling activity.

Along the front to the left stand pink, blue, white and yellow colonial mansions and town houses—freshly painted or dilapidated. The luscious colours of the tropical vegetation add to the dream-like quality of the scene. So does the **Igreja de Nossa Senhora da Conceição da Praia** (Church of Our Lady of the Immaculate Conception). This jewel of a church, constructed with Portuguese stone, dates back to the mid-18th century. Apart from "regular" services, the cult of the sea-goddess Iemanjá is celebrated here. Feast day: 8th December.

Now take the **Lacerda elevator** to ground level. This ancient contraption rattles down in all of a minute; it's slower than jumping, but safer! Step out of the lift and cross the road to **Praça Cairu** where you can join in all the fun of the **Mercado Modelo** (Model Market). Animated, colourful and crowded, the market has something for everybody, and you'll find it impossible not to make a purchase.

Jewellery, leather goods, hammocks, paintings, baskets, beads, clothes, musical instruments, dolls, souvenirs—and tasty snacks to keep your buying power up—are all very much on sale; plus a whole range of exotic paraphernalia, charms, herbs, spices and magic potions. And if Mercado Modelo isn't enough for you, browse your way through the produce market **Feira de São Joaquim** further along the seafront (a five-minute taxi ride away). Here, fresh fish, brilliant flowers, succulent vegetables, juicy fruit and assorted sounds give all five of your senses a treat.

From the bustle of the market-place make for the **Museu de Arte Sacra** (Sacred Art Museum) on rua do Sodré. A collection of beautiful and priceless works of sacred art from all Salvador has been gathered together here, in the old Carmelite convent of Santa Teresa. Painted tiles (azulejos), frescoes, sculptures, paintings,

statues illustrate the deepest beliefs of the first settlers.

Shops, offices, busy streets and residential areas characterize the upper city. But that doesn't mean that there are fewer sights. In fact many of the city's best examples of Baroque architecture will be found here, including the **Cathedral** (Sé) on Terreiro de Jesus. This marvellously well-preserved structure in fine Portuguese marble was erected by the Jesuits in 1672.

Awe-inspiring expression of Salvador's simple faith.

The paintings provide a history lesson in images. How—in a sense—the saints came marching into Bahia and with new names provided the basis for *candomblé,* the syncretic religion (combining Christianity and African spirit worship) which may not be quite orthodox, but certainly means something to the Bahians.

Cross the Terreiro de Jesus and walk down Praça Anchieta to visit the **Igreja de São Francisco.** The interior of this church is simply stunning. Gold leaf covers everything in sight —overwhelming ceilings, walls and altars. Jealously protected by Franciscan monks, the **cloister** has a collection of brilliant blue *azulejos.* (Only men are allowed access to the convent area.)

A few yards away from the convent you'll notice a remarkable **façade.** It is of the Igreja da Ordem Terceira de São Francisco. Curly stones, statues and incrustations fill the front, once again telling the familiar story—of a struggle, a hope, and a house for that hope.

Not far from the cathedral, a pretty district full of character is the **Largo do Pelourinho** (Place of the Pillory). Despite the shops, houses, restaurants and bustle, the very name of the sloping street will remind you of the infamous and brutal slave trade.

From Largo do Pelourinho make your way via rua L. Viana to the rua do Carmo. When the irritatingly stubborn Dutchmen who persistently tried to take the city in the 17th century were finally forced to capitulate, it was here, in the former Carmelite convent, that they reluctantly had to sign on the dotted line. See also the **church,** with its splendid sacristy and the **Museu do Carmo,** where there is a beautiful and impressive **statue** of the saviour as well as paintings and other objects of value.

You've now seen the principal treasures and sights that you are likely to be able to fit into a short visit to Salvador. There are nonetheless many other churches, forts, beaches and excursions for those with more time. Some of them:

Igreja de Nosso Senhor do Bonfim: An 18th-century church on the Itapagipe peninsula, famous chiefly for its January festival and miraculous cures.

Igreja de Boa Viagem *(cidade baixa):* Important place of worship, especially at the end of the year (January 1st procession).

Itapoã beach and the **Abaeté lagoon:** Out of town (on the north-east coast) but beautiful; the unique lagoon has black water and spooky legends.

Baía de Todos os Santos: From the port by Mercado Modelo trips out to the bay's islands and forts can be arranged.

North-east

RECIFE

Introduction

Built on the islands and peninsulas of two river deltas, sheltering behind the wall of reefs that gives it its name, Recife lays claim to the title "Venice of Brazil". But the resemblance to Venice ends with the bridges, waterways and Baroque churches, for this is a bustling harbour city, the larger-than-life capital of Pernambuco state, with modern tower blocks and a population of over one million.

History is ever present, much of it written in the buildings, especially the churches. There are 62 of them and many mark an episode in Recife's rebellious past, characterized by uprisings against the central government. Old colonial houses, ancient forts and monasteries, set in the luminous green of a luxuriant tropical vegetation, and miles of dazzling beaches bear out the words of one of Recife's own poets:

"Half of it stolen from the sea, the other half from the imagination".

Contrasting with the lively and brash atmosphere of Recife are the shaded cobbled streets and elegant houses of nearby Olinda, the ancient regional capital, today a national monument. Sister cities, they owed much of their prosperity in the 16th and 17th centuries to the sugar industry. Rich soil and an ideal tropical climate tempered by ocean breezes favoured the cultivation of sugar cane, and huge plantations *(fazendas)*, complete with slaves from Africa, grew up in the region. But competition from the Antilles and French and English West Indies threw the thriving industry into decline. Olinda, unlike Recife, never recovered, and the city has remained encapsulated in time.

The extrovert, affable *Recifenses* (as the people of Recife are called) have cultivated the Brazilian art of leisure. As the sun sinks behind the skyscrapers of the modern business centre, old town squares become the meeting points of artists, musicians and students, who perform impromptu street entertainments.

The streets come alive to the sound of folklore groups and Samba schools practising for the carnival—or any one of the half a dozen major festivals. And on the beach, pinpoints of fire and faintly heard rhythms signal the start of beach parties.

A Brief History

16th century	North-east Brazil is one of the first areas of the country to be settled by Europeans after the Portuguese discovery of Brazil in 1500. By the end of the 16th century the Portuguese establish sugar plantations and import African slaves. Recife, then known as Pernambuco, becomes the port of the colony established at nearby Olinda in 1537. In 1561 Recife is briefly occupied by French settlers. An English pirate, James Lancaster, plunders Recife in March 1595.
17th century	In 1630 the Dutch occupy Recife, destroy Olinda and rebuild it. They eventually extend their rule from the Amazon to the São Francisco River under the governorship of Maurice of Nassau, Prince of Orange. Recife, renamed Mauritzstad, becomes the Dutch capital in Brazil. When he leaves in 1644, the Dutch colonial effort crumbles and the Portuguese drive them out in 1654 after the Battle of Guararapes.
18th century	In 1710, conflict breaks out between the planters of Olinda and the merchants of Recife. When the fighting is over, Recife expands inland and bridges are built from the islands to the mainland. The town enjoys a century of growth based on sugar exports.
19th century	On March 6, 1817, a republican revolt breaks out in Recife and the governor is forced to flee to Rio. In June, Portuguese rule is restored, and the new governor, Luís do Rego Barreto imposes harsh military rule. A rebel army captures Luís do Rego and forces the signing of a convention in October 1820, giving Recife virtual independence well before the rest of the country. In 1825 imperial troops crush a republican revolt in Recife against the rule of Emperor Pedro I. The next 100 years are marked by a number of revolts against central rule.
20th century	In 1911 a popular uprising overthrows the governor. In 1930 revolutionary forces gather in Recife to march on the capital for the coup that brings Dr. Getúlio Vargas to power. He rules as dictator until 1945. The liberal republic restored in 1946 lasts until military intervention in 1964. Recife harbour is expanded and modernized.

Folklore

Recife is noted for its special folklore traditions, with origins in the cults of bygone African civilizations.

There are strong traces of African culture in the *mamulengo*, a theatrical performance about good versus evil, featuring wooden dolls, or the *bumba-meu-boi*, an act about the life and death of the ox.

Carnival here has yet to reach the super-operatic proportions of the Rio and Salvador spectaculars, but some say the Recife carnival is the best and most spontaneous in Brazil. Supporters of the Olinda carnival will claim theirs is the most intimate and genuine.

It is underscored by the particular, heady rhythm of the *frevo*, which leaves participants free to indulge in extraordinary, acrobatic dance interpretations—at times so complicated that the dancer risks losing his balance.

Particular to Recife is the *maracatú* dance, a glittering conga of music and allegorical figures that weaves its way from church to church.

Occasionally you will see a weirdly costumed figure dancing between the traffic, a tiny umbrella held aloft to create an illusion of balance—a one-man carnival momentarily creating a little world of pleasure.

Sightseeing

The old part of Recife is relatively small and easy to visit. It is divided into three districts—Recife district, on its own island, and Santo Antônio and São José sharing the peninsula of another island.

The main attraction of the old town is its churches, enough for the most ardent churchgoer, but there is one that you should not miss—the **Capela Dourada** in Santo Antônio district. It's a Baroque dream in gold, built at the end of the 17th century to show the world that this colonial outpost could somehow rival the architectural splendours of Europe.

Attached to the "Golden Chapel" is a small **museum** of religious art. Next door is the **São Francisco Monastery** with its church of **Santo Antônio** (1606)—the oldest in Recife. It's worth visiting for the beautiful Portuguese tiles.

Nearby, overlooking a square shaded with palm trees, the **Teatro Santa Isabel** (Saint Isabel Theatre) was inaugurated in 1850 but destroyed by fire in 1869. Restored and reopened by 1876, it has been a place of both artistic and political import—a plaque in the main corridor reads: "Here we won the cause for the abolition of slavery. Joaquim Nabuco".

Crossing the modern, sky-scraperlined Avenida Guararapes—the business centre of Recife—you come to Rua Nova and the Church of **Nossa Senhora da Conceição dos Militares** (1708) with its grand ceiling and an 18th-century primitive mural depicting the Battle of Guararapes.

From here you enter the São José district. Head for the Church of **São Pedro dos Clérigos** behind whose beautifully sculpted façade lie fine wood carvings and an unusual trompe-l'oeil ceiling that is unique in Brazil.

The square here forms the heart of the artists' and intellectuals' quarter.

The São José quarter hides a warren of market streets jammed full of traders, musicians, mothers and babies, culminating in the iron hall of the **central market.** It's a photogenic display of colour and noise, spiced by the competing pungency of fish, leather, fruit and drains.

Take time to visit the **Sugar**

It's carnival every day in Pernambuco when you're young.

Museum on Avenida 17 de Agosto, a fascinating insight into the days when sugar cane was the raison d'être of this region.

Cross over the Mauricio de Nassau Bridge to Recife island. The church here worth visiting is the **Madre de Deus** with its Baroque wood carvings and splendid high altar and sacristy.

One of the most imposing remains of Dutch rule is the **Forte de Brum** (Fort Brum) on the northern end of Recife island. It was begun in 1629 by the Portuguese in a vain effort to secure the defence of Olinda. The Dutch completed it in 1631. From here you can view the **harbour** protected by its reef.

One of the top attractions of Recife is its dazzling six-mile-long beach, **Boa Viagem**. Fringed with coconut palms, it's the weekend parade ground of the *Recifenses*.

Excursions

Olinda

"O linda!" (Oh beautiful) exclaimed Duarte Coelho Pereira in 1535 when he arrived at the site of the future settlement of Olinda, 4 miles (6 km.) from Recife. Today this ancient colonial capital, the cradle of Brazilian culture, is a national monument.

Walk through the narrow streets to the cathedral square, the **Alto da Sé,** where you will be rewarded with a wonderful panorama of Olinda, its white-washed and pastel-coloured buildings half submerged by the palms of tropical gardens, with the endless blue of the Atlantic beyond.

Local crafts are for sale in the square and nearby is the **Museum of Art** and the old **Slave Market** (Mercado da Ribeira), where scenes of young and old at work on their exquisite woodcarving cannot quite lay to rest the images of the cruel past.

Igaraçu and Itamaracá

Itamaracá, 29 miles (46 km.) from Recife, is a lovely island linked to the mainland by a bridge. It is known for its deserted, palm-fringed beaches, the ruins of old naval buildings, the first sugar mills of Brazil and **Fort Orange,** built by the Dutch in 1631.

Igaraçu, on the mainland, was the first European settlement in Pernambuco, founded in 1535. It has a remarkable architectural heritage and claims to have the first church built in Brazil.

North-east

FORTALEZA

Introduction

Capital of the state of Ceará, Fortaleza is known as "the Princess of the North", the key city of Brazil's Costa do Sol—Sunshine Coast—with its miles of superb beaches shaded by coconut palms and lapped by the rolling waves of the Atlantic Ocean.

The city is laid out like a chessboard with its wide avenues crossing each other at right angles. Large parks and squares and the pastel-coloured or whitewashed buildings inspire a feeling of light and space.

The beaches range from the deserted to the noisy playgrounds of some of the world's most handsome people. The Cearans, whose ethnic origins have been blurred by the generations, are noted for their courage, tenacity and intelligence.

These are the people who spend days at sea on nothing more than a few logs lashed together. Known as *jangadas,* these crude fishing craft, driven by graceful triangular sails, have become the symbol of Ceará. The *jangadeiros* are the maritime equivalent of the cattle droving *vaqueiros* of the hinterland, or the *seringueiros*—rubber tappers who confront the steamy jungles of the interior armed with little more than a sharp knife.

Fortaleza is the centre of a rich and varied craftsmanship, particularly of lacemaking and delicate embroidery. It is also an artistic centre that gives inspiration to strolling guitar players as they sing the folk ballads of the region, the *literatura de cordel.*

A Brief History

16th century	In February 1500, three months before the Portuguese discovery of Brazil, a Spanish explorer, Vicente Yáñez Pinzón, is said to have landed in the Fortaleza area. Later in the century, the economic potential of sugar cane becomes apparent and thousands of Africans are brought to the region as slaves.
17th century	Pero Coelho de Souza builds a fort on the site of Fortaleza in 1603 as a base for his unsuccessful expeditions into the interior. In 1612, a settlement and Fort São Sebastiano are established by Martin Soares Moreno.

The Dutch seize the fort in 1637, and in a second invasion in 1649, build Fort Schonenborch as a base for silver expeditions into the interior. The Dutch withdraw in 1654 after their defeat at Recife. The Portuguese rebuild the Dutch fortifications, renaming them Nossa Senhora da Assunção, and settlements grow up around the complex. Jesuit missionaries leave from here to convert the Indians of the interior.

18th century	By 1726, the fortress and the surrounding town become the provincial capital with the name Cidade de Fortaleza de Nova Bragança. Despite its favourable situation, Fortaleza never manages to compete as a trading post and it is only in the following century that it begins to grow and prosper.
19th century	In 1824, Fortaleza joins other north-eastern towns, including Recife, in the shortlived Equatorial Confederation—a rebel movement opposed to the rule of Emperor Pedro I. Towards the end of the century, Fortaleza becomes one of the first towns to abolish slavery.
20th century	The government uses force to put down a religiously inspired movement led by Father Cicero. Fortaleza, a leading world producer of spiny lobsters, finds itself at the centre of the so-called Lobster War, a fishing dispute with France.

Sightseeing

Practically every visitor to Fortaleza ends up in jail sooner or later, for it is the old city jail that has become the cultural and social centre of the town.

The people of Fortaleza are proud of their jail—now known as the **Tourist Centre**—which has been recently converted into a museum, an art gallery and a shopping centre for the arts and crafts of the region. Wardens and convicts have been replaced by shopkeepers and their customers, the rattle of chains has given way to the ring of cash registers, and the prisoners' exercise yard is now a children's playground.

You may prefer the freedom of shopping in the shady labyrinth of the **Central Mar-**

ket, where the stalls overflow with medicinal herbs and essences, fabrics, souvenirs and local produce, including cashew nuts, of which this region is the main producer.

Opposite the market is the new **Cathedral,** built of concrete in neo-classical style. It is famous for its stained glass windows.

To get away from the bustle of the market, walk further into town where you will find the **Cidade da Criança**—a pretty park with a lake and a zoo especially designed to appeal to children.

Near the park, the **Historical and Anthropological Museum** houses an imposing collection of arms, stamps, paintings and prehistoric implements, as well as a curious exhibit—the remains of the aircraft in which President Castello Branco (1964–67) lost his life. Mementos of the president can be seen at his **mausoleum** next to the state government building.

There is always an architectural surprise in a Brazilian town, and Fortaleza's is the **José de Alencar Theatre,** on your way back to the city centre from the museum. It's an example of pure art nouveau style and boasts a simple system of practical air conditioning: it has no side walls.

Nothing remains of the original Dutch fort in the city centre, but on its site is built the 17th-century **Forte Nossa Senhora da Assunção.**

Excursions

If they are not at work, the Fortalezans are on the beach —especially on **Iracema** beach, the nearest to the city. There are finer beaches further to the south, especially the dune-covered **Futuro** beach five miles (8 km.) away by bus and **Volta da Jurema.**

The coastline curves round further, offering a range of tempting beaches that stretch almost to the easternmost point of Brazil. The often-deserted white sands of **Capanga** can be reached by bus from Cascavel, to the south-east. Fish are plentiful and varied—not far away, a river flows into the Atlantic and trips with the *jangadeiros* can be arranged.

A pretty drive south-west from Fortaleza takes you up into the mountains for a change, to the **Serra de Maranguape.** The view from there across to the city 19 miles (31 km) away, and the accompanying tropical vegetation, make picnicking a delightful prospect.

North

THE AMAZON

Introduction

Mightiest of all rivers, the Amazon flows through the last great wilderness on earth, an area of virgin jungle the size of Europe, still largely unexplored. In the forest depths, Stone-Age Indian tribes hunt with blow-pipe and poisoned arrow; jaguars, tapirs and giant anteaters roam the interior. Even for the tourist, cushioned by comfort, travelling the Amazon is an adventure.

Rising amid the snows of the Andes in Peru, the Amazon winds across almost the whole width of the South-American continent, through Brazil, to the Atlantic.

Geologists believe the river once flowed into the Pacific, but that the rise of the Andes tipped it to the east, turning the plain into a great inland sea until the river found an outlet into the Atlantic Ocean. Every year, when the Amazon bursts its banks, the waters spread over hundreds of square miles of floodplain, recreating a freshwater sea that inundates the lowland forest.

In this humid, hothouse climate, just below the equator, plants and animals have evolved over millions of years in a profusion and variety unmatched elsewhere. It is estimated that the Amazon basin contains more than 10 percent of all the world's plant and animal species.

In this secluded world, several hundred Indian tribes held undisturbed sway, until the Europeans arrived.

But until the past 30 years, neither the Indians, with their shifting cultivation, nor the European settlers, clinging to the river edges, had made any real mark on the great rainforest. Today, for the first time, the impact of man is becoming evident.

From the air, the jungle still seems limitless, a carpet of green, broken by the occasional glint of a river or an oxbow lake.

But exploitation is already in full swing. To the south of the river, the Trans-Amazonian Highway cuts a wide gash through the forest from east to west, along the edge of the plain. Other highways strike south from Belém to Brazil's capital, Brasilia, and north from Manaus to the Venezuelan border.

Oil is being drilled in the upper Amazon basin, near Iquitos in Peru. Surveys have pinpointed vast mineral wealth along the river's tributaries in Brazil.

Up the River

Belém, gateway to the Amazon, lies on the southern bank of a branch of the delta, the Rio do Pará.

Near Belém, the Amazon is joined by the first of its big tributaries, the **Tocantins,** which traverses a region rich in minerals.

Opposite the city, the huge island of **Marajó**, bigger than Switzerland, blocks the mouth of the Amazon like a cork in a bottleneck. The first part of your cruise leads through the

fascinating narrows round the south of the island, known as the **Breves**, where the jungle crowds in on either side and fishermen's houses on stilts overhang the banks.

Once you reach the mainstream of the Amazon, the river opens out to a width of several miles. No wonder the early Portuguese called it *O Rio Mar*, the River Sea; at times the shores almost disappear.

After the forests of the Amazon delta, swampy marshlands and grassy meadows line the northern bank, with ranges of hills behind them. Near here, the Amazon is

An Amazon settlement—not much has changed over the years.

joined from the north by the **Jari River**. A giant onslaught on the jungle is in progress here, launched by American industrialist Daniel K. Ludwig, to clear a 5,600 square mile (14,000 sq. km.) area for agriculture and industry.

From the south, the **Rio Xingu** flows into the Amazon, a wild river flowing turbulently through dense jungle. In its upper reaches a huge reserve has been established for the remnants of 16 Indian tribes uprooted and dispossessed by development plans.

Two days up the Amazon from Belém, you reach Santarém, a busy little port thronged with fishing boats and dugout canoes, at the junction with the **Tapajós River**. The discovery of gold along the Tapajós has brought a mini-boom to this small town of half a million people, originally settled by soldiers from the disbanded Confederate army after the American Civil War.

A little way up the Tapajós you'll find the unspoiled, lovely beach of **Alter do Chão**, with safe waters ideal for a swim, on the edge of the jungle.

Manaus stands just up the Rio Negro from the conflu-

How the Amazon got its Name

The ancient Greeks believed there was a race of female warriors living near the Black Sea, whom they called the Amazons. The name comes from a Greek word meaning "without a breast", since the girls were said to have their right breast burnt off, the better to draw the bow.

In 1541, Friar Gaspar de Caravajal, chronicler of Orellana's expedition, claimed to have seen tall, fair Indian women warriors leading an attack with bows and arrows along the great river they were exploring. Till then they had called the river the Marañon ("That which only God can unravel"). Thenceforth it was known as River of the Amazons. Although subsequent expeditions never sighted any such warlike women, the name stuck.

ence, a modern city and deep-water port in the heart of the wilderness, 1,000 miles (1,600 km.) from the sea.

The upper reaches of the Amazon beyond Manaus are particularly interesting, as the river, on this stretch called the **Solimões**, narrows between dense walls of jungle. Indian settlements can be seen along the banks.

The Indians

The dense Amazon interior, known also as the Green Hell.

When the first Europeans reached the Amazon in the 16th century, the number of Indians is estimated to have been as high as 3 million. Friar Gaspar de Caravajal, travelling with a Spanish expedition in 1541, wrote that Indian villages lined many parts of the river "each not a crossbow shot from the next".

Today there remain fewer than 250,000 Indians in Brazil, of whom perhaps 50,000 still live in the jungle in the Amazon basin.

They hunt and fish with bow and arrow. Apart from manioc, which they treat by scraping, washing and squeezing to remove the poisonous prussic acid, they grow chilis, yams, papayas, bananas, peanuts and beans in jungle clearings; they also eat wild nuts, fruits and berries, fish, game and insects.

They resent and will often kill intruders. Their *shamans* still conduct rites to protect the group against sorcerers. Some tribes ensure the contin-

Amazing Amazon

From its source in the Andes to its mouth on the Atlantic, the Amazon extends 4,000 miles (6,440 km.), the second longest river in the world after the Nile.

It has the largest volume of any river, discharging into the Atlantic 25 times the amount disgorged by the Nile. Such is its force that the fresh water pumped into the sea spreads 100 miles (160 km.) from the land.

The Amazon is fed by 1,000 rivers; seven of them—the Japurá, Juruá, Madeira, Negro, Purus, Tocantins and Xingu are each more than 1,000 miles (1,600 km.) long.

It is the deepest river on earth, measuring in places 250 feet (76 m.), yet its bottom is almost flat, descending towards the ocean at a gradient of only one-quarter of an inch per mile (about 1 cm. per km.) over most of the basin.

The Amazon basin covers 2,720,000 square miles (7 million sq. km.), nearly twice the area drained by any other river in the world.

ued survival of their dead by eating their ashes, mingled with boiled banana.

Even today, some of the Amazonian Indians share with primitive peoples in Asia the use of the blow-pipe and the penis-sheath, suggesting a common ancestry.

The **Waimiri-Atroari** live north of Manaus, where their tribal lands are cut by a new road running north to the Venezuelan border. They remain fiercely remote and over the past two decades have killed 20 people who entered their territory, including a missionary.

The **Yanomamo**, or "the fierce people", inhabit the forest up the Rio Negro, north-west of Manaus, near the Venezuelan frontier. Largest of the remaining Indian tribes, numbering several thousand, they speak a language unlike that of any other group. Their staple is the banana, rather than manioc. Little sticks thrust through the nose and round the mouth provide ornament. Their enemies called them the Waika or "bad".

South of the Amazon, many of the remaining tribes have been regrouped in the Xingu reserve, including the **Kren-Akroare**, reduced to only 79 members by inter-tribal warfare and disease.

The **Urubu**, south-east of Belém, took their name from the local black vulture.

North

BELÉM

Introduction

It stands, hot, humid and sultry, just south of the equator, on the threshold of the Amazonian basin, the greatest jungle and river area in the world. Its back garden contains 18,000 species of plants—three-quarters of those known to man. It is haunted by legends of lost gold and steeped in the mysteries of magic. Small wonder that Belém is a magnet for tourists seeking a taste of the Amazon adventure.

Capital of Pará state, Belém is a rather confused and sprawling city of contrasts. Skyscrapers loom awkwardly over trim colonial buildings of slightly faded splendour, remnants of the days when the Dutch tiled façades were painted to match the colours of equatorial fruits and birds. The tropical temperament is noticeable everywhere; it lulls you into a leisurely pace of life common in this part of the world.

The inhabitants of Belém have been described as more sombre than southern Brazilians. This impression is enhanced by the mysticism of the local *mestizos*, who produce and sell magic remedies in a colourful—and sometimes grisly—fashion.

You won't find summer and winter here. Belém's calendar follows the pattern of the rain. Don't be put off when you're told that 245 days of the year are wet. This often means just a brief mid-afternoon deluge, which can be predicted so accurately that Belém businessmen regularly fix appointments for "before" or "after".

The daily downpour at least keeps the evenings cool and the jungle in bloom, as well as helping the Amazon supply a quarter of the world's fresh water and a third of its oxygen. A hundred years ago, it also supplied the world's rubber, putting Belém firmly on the map as economic capital of northern Brazil. The city's cluttered port still controls the region's commerce and is a natural embarkation point for river and jungle exploration.

A Brief History

15th century	The newly discovered lands in the Americas and the East are officially divided between Spain and Portugal, when they sign the Treaty of Tordesillas in 1494. The Americas are allotted to Spain, but the dividing line

passes just east of the Amazon delta, giving Portugal a claim to Brazil.

16th century	In 1500, the year Brazil is discovered, the Spanish explorer Vicente Yañez Pinzón encounters members of the ancient Tupi and Aruaque tribes near the site of Belém. Forty years later fellow countryman Francisco de Orellano tells of a 2,000-mile river journey and battles against the fabled women warriors, the Amazons, riding white horses.
17th century	Two hundred Portuguese soldiers land in Guajará Bay to expel English, French and Dutch invaders, and the fortified settlement of Feliz Lusitânia (Happy Portugal) is established. In 1616 it takes the name Nossa Senhora de Belém do Grão-Pará (Our Lady of Bethlehem on the Great Pará River)—Belém for short. The area of Pará becomes a captaincy in 1652. Sugar trading develops, and in 1655 Belém receives city status.
18th century	Cattle ranching spreads. The first latex is exported through Belém to France in 1735. In 1772 Pará is separated from Maranhão, and Belém becomes state capital.
19th century	The people of Belém resist independence and are forced to pay homage to Dom Pedro I in 1823, a year after he declares himself Emperor of Brazil. In 1835 they join the Cabanagem Revolution. Within 12 months the resistance is crushed, with many killed. In 1859, an English naturalist catalogues 14,712 animal species in the Amazon basin—8,000 of them unknown to science. Rubber is exported regularly, following Goodyear's discovery of vulcanization in 1848. The production of pneumatic tyres from 1888 onwards assures Belém's prosperity for the next 40 years.
20th century	Belém's population doubles in ten years, to 192,000 in 1907. Then comes the crash. Rubber tree seeds are smuggled out, and by 1913, Southeast Asia is producing more latex than Brazil. The market collapses, thousands of Europeans leave and Belém sinks back into relative obscurity. Later, the government invests in mineral projects. Belém is linked by road to the capital, Brasília.

Sightseeing

One of Belém's most fascinating sights is the **Mercado de Ver-o-Peso** (See-the-Weight Market), alongside the docks on Largo do Relógio. Go as early as possible. Once you've explored the huge food halls, browse through the more unusual offerings: crocodile-tooth rosaries, bird skeletons, leopard tails, dolphin eyes, dried boa constrictor heads... you'll find magic charms and potions to cure—or cause—almost anything.

Afterwards, catch the Souza bus as far as the **Bosque Rodrigues Alves**, an impressive jungle park in Avenida Almirante Barroso. It's set in an area of luxuriant vegetation preserved since the days of the rubber boom.

Beyond Belém's skyscraper horizon, the start of the unknown.

You can get the same bus back as far as the **Museu Emílio Goeldi** in Avenida Magalhães Barata, an anthropology museum offering a pictorial insight into the tribes of the Amazon. It has Indian artefacts and weapons, an extensive library, a zoo and the largest collection of tropical plants in the world. Both park and museum enable you to venture as close to the jungle as you could comfortably wish—with alligators, anacondas and other wild animals you could miss during a river trip.

Next to the zoo is the **Paraíso das Tartarugas** (Turtle Paradise), refuge for several thousand of the species who would otherwise end up on the menu as one of the region's principal gastronomic delights.

From here it's worth walking. Go west along the avenue to **Praça Justo Chermont**, where you can take in the imposing stained-glass windows and marble of the **Basílica de Nossa Senhora de Nazaré**, built in 1909 as a replica of St. Paul's, Rome. It is here, on the second Sunday of October, that one of Brazil's religious festivals begins. The *Procissão do Círio de Nazaré* (Procession of the Nazareth Candle) is a 15-day event that

attracts half a million people. Along from the Edifício Manuel Pinto de Silva is the **municipal theatre** *(Teatro da Paz)*, unmistakable with its Neoclassic marble columns, sculptures and crystal mirrors that reflect the extravagances of the rubber era. The theatre was opened in 1878, after almost ten years of painstaking planning and construction. Pavlova danced there.

Follow Avenida Presidente Vargas, which leads to the

port. Turn down Rua Santo Antônio and Rua João Alfredo, two interesting streets that take you through the commercial centre. You'll see Belém's oldest church, the **Igreja de Nossa Senhora das Mercês**, which dates from the late 17th century. Carry on, and you come to Praça Dom Pedro II, and the Prefeitura Municipal. Beyond is the imposing Baroque façade of the **cathedral**, built in 1748 and restored in 1887. The pope sent Carrara marble for the altar. Opposite is the 18th-century **Igreja Santo Alexandre**, now a museum of religious art.

Close to the cathedral is Belém's "foundation stone" —**Forte do Castelo**, the original fort, which today bears the name of the Portuguese captain who had it built. Climb up to the cannons at the top for a strategic—and panoramic—view of Guajará Bay.

Excursions

If you just want to head for the nearest beach, **Outeiro** is an hour away by bus and ferry on one of the 2,000 islands spread across the Pará estuary. A dozen other sandy beaches lie in romantic isolation on the **Ilha do Mosqueiro**. The bus journey takes an hour and a half, and is a popular Sunday excursion for local people.

Further afield, and definitely worth a visit, is **Marajó**, the vast island straddling the mouth of the Amazon. It is known as the cradle of the Marajoara civilization, whose descendants live today as they did centuries ago. The island is renowned for its 700,000 buffalo. You can also see thousands of tropical birds and—if you're lucky—sea turtles laying their eggs in the sand. Allow four hours by boat, or 40 minutes by air-taxi.

Fish that Feed in the Forest
Every year, when the rivers of the Amazon basin break their banks, fish swim through the forests, feeding on dropped fruits. Seed pods explode in the sun, fall into the water and are gulped down by the fish, including the *tambaqui*, the most important commercial fish in the Amazon.

Fish-eating fish, such as the piranha and catfish, fatten in turn on the fruit-eaters. At the same time the fish help the renewal of the forests by dispersing the seeds. This remarkable interaction between fish and forest also benefits the local people for whom fish is a major source of protein.

North

MANAUS

Introduction

Manaus glitters like a mirage against the emerald green of the jungle, a surprise modern city and deep-water port in the heart of the wilderness, 1,000 miles (1,600 km.) up the Amazon from the sea.

Here, where the dark waters of the Rio Negro join the flow of the world's mightiest river, lies the trade centre of Brazil's vast new development plans for the Amazon basin.

Once a rubber boom town, then derelict for almost half a century, Manaus is once again on the upsurge of a wave of prosperity. Capital of the vast Amazonas state (Brazil's largest), it stands in a key position at the crossroads of air and river routes and of the network of highways now being slashed through the Amazonian forests. The city lies midway between the mouth of the Amazon on the Atlantic and the Peruvian river port of Iquitos, nearly a whole continent away upstream. Even at Manaus the Amazon is still 7 miles (11 km.) wide.

From the riverside floating docks (floating because the Amazon can rise as much as 90 feet [30 m.] in flood season), timber, jute, pepper, nuts and rubber are shipped down the Amazon in ocean-going vessels.

For the tourist, Manaus is a good take-off point for travel to the upper reaches of the Amazon and its tributaries, for hunting and fishing expeditions, and for visits to jungle lodges where tribal Indians will demonstrate their skill with the blow-pipe and bow.

Starting as a small fortress outpost of the early Portuguese colonists, Manaus burst into fame in the late 19th century with the sudden boom in rubber. Adventurers made fortunes overnight from latex tapped from jungle rubber trees and exported to North America and Europe for the burgeoning cycle and automobile industries.

Rubber barons, waxing rich on their world monopoly, built fabulous mansions, embellished with wrought-iron, crystal and porcelain from Europe, and added tramways and electric lighting to the city streets.

Their greatest pride was the magnificent Opera House (still standing), built out of rubber taxes, where singers and ballet troupes from Europe came to perform before an audience decked out in full evening dress and diamonds.

But rival rubber plantations started up in South-east Asia. The fleeting golden days were over. Manaus fell into decay.

The government set the city on the road to recovery in 1967 by declaring it a free port, thereby attracting new industry as well as tourists eager to buy duty-free luxury goods. Oil from the newly discovered fields in Peru was brought to Manaus for refining. Within a few years the population doubled and is now heading for 1 million.

To the north a new road cuts through the jungle to the cattle grasslands of Roraima state and on to the Venezuelan frontier. South of the Amazon, opposite Manaus, a trunk route is being developed, linking up with the Trans-Amazonian Highway and with the capital, Brasilia, 1,600 miles (2,600 km.) away.

Manaus is a patchwork of high-rise buildings, pedestrian shopping precincts, modern hotels, old world mansions and *favelas* (shanty towns) of thatch, wood and tin. The city is criss-crossed by waterways, known as *igarapés* or canoe channels, which run into the Rio Negro.

The people are a cross-section of the world—Portuguese and other Europeans, Amazonian Indians, black descendants of African slaves, peoples of mixed race. The universal language is Portuguese, but you'll find Indians still speaking some of the 150 tribal tongues.

Manaus is an isolated foothold of the modern world in the wilds of the Amazon. On all sides, the jungle presses in. Primitive tribes still live in the forests to the north. Jaguars and giant anacondas inhabit the interior. Exploitation of the region has indeed begun, but it will be many years before it is fully tamed.

A Brief History

40,000–30,000 B.C	Stone-Age Indian tribes, migrating from North and Central America, settle in the Amazon region, living as hunter-gatherers.
3000 B.C.	The Indians begin cultivating manioc as a staple and become agriculturists as well as hunters.
16th century A.D.	Spanish explorers first sight the mouth of the Amazon in 1500. In 1541–1542, a Spanish commander, Francisco

de Orellana, crosses the Andes from the Pacific side, descends the Napo tributary with 57 followers and travels down the Amazon, alternately harassed and helped by Indians, past the site where Manaus now stands, and on to the Atlantic.

17th–18th centuries

In 1635, Portuguese explorer Pedro Teixeira travels up the Amazon, from Belém to the foot of the Andes. In 1669, the Portuguese establish a fort and trading settlement on the site of present-day Manaus and call it Fortaleza da Barra, from the *barra* (sandbar) at the mouth of the Rio Negro. Sailing vessels carry cargoes of cacao seeds (for cocoa production) and turtle oil down the river for export.

19th century

Brazil proclaims its independence from Portugal in 1822. In 1851 Barra changes its name to Manáos (now Manaus), after the name of a local Indian tribe, and becomes capital of Amazonas state. The first steamships ply between Belém and Manaus, cutting the voyage from six weeks to one week. Rubber exploitation begins.

20th century

Manaus rivals European cities in the elegance of its buildings and the luxurious life of its rubber barons. The city decays with the collapse of the rubber boom, but revives when the Brazilian government declares it a free port and grants tax concessions. With the expansion of air and river traffic and the development of road communications, tourism increases.

Sightseeing

The one sight not to be missed is the Opera House, the **Teatro Amazonas**, usually floodlit at night, which dominates the heart of the city. You will marvel the more at this magnificently Baroque building when you realize that the entire structure with its contents was imported brick by brick, piece by piece, from Europe 100 years ago, when the Amazon region had scarcely been explored.

The green-blue and gold tiles of the imposing dome came from Alsace-Lorraine, the marble from Italy, the interior furnishings from France. It was opened in 1896 at the height of the rubber boom, restored to its former grandeur in 1974 and is now used for occasional performances.

Standing on a balustraded terrace, the Opera House is approached by a double sweep of curved steps.

The interior of the theatre is all plush, mahogany and gilt.

In the centre of the geometrically patterned paved square outside stands a flamboyant **Monument to Navigation**, resting on the iron prows of ships

The Opera House—echo of a glorious era in the Amazon.

82

setting out to discover the continents.

The Opera House is the most notable building in Manaus, far outclassing the Jesuit-built **cathedral** on a nearby hill. But among the modern office blocks you can still find some of the gracious **mansions** of the rubber barons, elegantly faced with wrought-iron grilles and balconies (all imported from Europe, of course).

Go down to the waterfront to watch the bustle of river traffic, where merchant ships tie up at the **floating docks**, alongside the old-fashioned double-decker riverboats and frail covered crafts with outboard motors, in which whole families sling their hammocks athwart the hull for a voyage lasting maybe several days.

Behind the docks stands the **Customs House**, of imported Scottish stone, and the **City Market** (*Mercado municipal*) where you can buy almost anything, from food and magic potions to tethered parrots and brilliant little birds, sadly caged.

Visit the **Indian Museum** at the Salesian Catholic school to see Indian costumes, weapons and artefacts.

The city has two **zoos**, one in the centre, and the other, with a much larger selection of animals, established by the army at their jungle training headquarters, further out of the city.

Excursions

Unless you have already seen it on your way up-river by boat, you will want to take a trip to view the **Wedding of the Waters**, where the acid black Rio Negro and the yellow nutrient-rich flood of the Solimões flow side by side for some 50 miles (80 km.), slowly intermingling.

Other boat trips on the Rio Negro will take you through narrow streams overhung by tropical greenery alive with birds, past waterside fishermen's huts on stilts, or to a lake to see the giant *Victoria amazonica* waterlilies, with round leaves like huge dinner plates, reaching more than 6 feet (2 m.) across.

About 60 miles (100 km.) above Manaus, where the river Negro broadens out to a width of 12 miles (20 km.), are the **Anavilhanas Islands**, the largest freshwater archipelago in the world, long ribbons of forested islands, where all hunting, fishing and forestry is banned.

Centre-West

BRASÍLIA

Introduction

Brasília is a world apart, like no other capital city anywhere. Everything about it is unique. It started life in 1956 when materials and workers were parachuted on to a deserted, dusty plateau, with instructions to build a new capital for Brazil halfway between the Amazon jungle and the fleshpots of Rio. Just four years later, it was ready.

The capital of the country had always been on the coast—first at Bahia, then Rio—but, for more than two centuries, Brazilian philosophers had been advocating a move inland as the only way to develop the whole country. But it was not until 1956 that President Juscelino Kubitschek (JK as he was known) won unanimous parliamentary approval for his bill creating a bureaucracy empowered to plan and finally construct the new city.

The futuristic metropolis was the audacious enterprise of Brazilian architect Oscar Niemeyer and urbanist Lúcio Costa. Landscape architect Roberto Burle Marx was assigned to bring life to the spaces between the monuments.

At first the city was hailed as a real-life utopia, but mass migration exceeded all imagined targets, bringing the population up to 1.2 million (most of whom live in satellite shanty towns) and putting paid to the planners' dream. Adjustments and compromises have had to be fitted into the idealistic pilot plan; for instance, traffic lights—originally deemed superfluous in the brilliantly designed highway network—are now necessary on some streets to cope with the proliferating number of cars.

But it's still a fascinating place. The upside-down arches of the presidential palace, the startling inverted dome of the congress building and the thrusting spikes atop the surprising subterranean cathedral make all who visit Brasília marvel at the architects' inspired ingenuity.

The man-made eccentricities of this model city (which include an artificial lake), are set off by the rusty red of the soil, which tints the bases of the grey concrete structures. And at this height—the city is 3,700 feet (1,150 m.) above sea level!—the sky appears above you like an immense blue dome, turning purple at dusk in the afterglow of the huge, panoramic sunset over the city and the wilderness beyond.

Even if you decide that Brasília is not the ideal place to live after all, you can't help being captivated by its sheer audacity and vision. And if it has its imperfections now, that only serves to make it a bit more human.

A Brief History

16th century	Following Brazil's discovery, a vast stretch of land—today's Goiás state—remains a wilderness as settlers choose the coast to grow sugar cane.
17th–18th centuries	With population of the New World in full swing, some settlers decide to explore the interior from São Paulo. In central Minas Gerais, gold first, then diamonds, are discovered, prompting a great rush in the early 18th

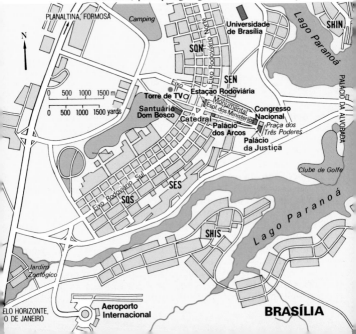

	century. Sugar loses importance, gold and diamonds dominate the country, with Rio de Janeiro springing up as an outlet for the industry.
19th century	Coffee becomes the new boom product as the other minerals fade away. In the mid-19th century, immigrants from Europe pour into Brazil's prosperous coastal towns and cities, many cultivating their own farms and plantations. Slave trading is abolished in 1850. In 1891—two years after the proclamation in Rio de Janeiro of a federal republic by Marshal Deodoro da Fonseca—the Constitution pledges to build a new capital on the central plateau.
20th century	Under the presidency of Juscelino Kubitschek in 1956, it is finally decided to decentralize Brazil's coastal concentration with a new, modern, inland capital city, some 600 miles (1,000 km.) north-west of Rio. Four hard years later, on April 21, 1960, Brasília becomes the new capital and the most modern city in the world. The government moves from Rio to Brasília, even though the city is still "rough at the edges". The city today houses some 411,000 people, while shanty towns spread around the city are home to a further ¾ million. Frequent air-links with Rio encourage tourism.

Sightseeing

Lúcio Costa's conception of Brasília began as a simple cross on a piece of paper and evolved into a curved axis crossing a straight line, like the wings and fuselage of an aeroplane. The straight line, called the **Eixo Monumental** (Monumental Axis), is the area set aside for government and culture. The intersecting arc, called the Eixo Rodoviário (Highway Axis), slices through the housing districts, which are divided into "superblocks", self-sufficient mini-neighbourhoods. The "wings" and "body" intersect, on separate levels, at the Bus Terminal (Estação Rodoviária), around which are situated business and entertainment facilities.

Brasilienses (residents of the capital) have to know dozens of abbreviations and acronyms: SHIN means North Individual Housing Sector and SQS means Superquadra Sul, or South Superblock.

Later on the agenda: Brasília's **cathedral**, actually far bigger than it looks, for only the cupola is above ground. The gracefully curved struts of the conical superstructure form one of the capital's favourite landmarks. Inside the cathedral, natural sunlight cheers (and sometimes overheats) the circular nave. Three large aluminium angels float near the ceiling, adding to the airy charm of a thoroughly unconventional church.

The cathedral is right beside the Monumental Axis leading to the area of the **Esplanada dos Ministérios,** each ministry in its own identical, rather Kafkaesque glass box. Students of government will not be surprised to learn that all the ministries have now outgrown their headquarters; luxurious new annexes have been built to accommodate the swarms of additional public servants.

At the far end of the Monumental Axis, the **Praça dos Três Poderes** (Square of the Three Powers) sees the confrontation, or convergence, of the executive, legislative and judicial branches of the federal government. The architecture here reaches its apex, as if each of the Three Powers were striving to achieve the

Arches and angles make Brasília an architect's dream.

Tourists are taken through a typical superblock, with its own recreational and shopping facilities and school. They visit one of the simple churches built in the pioneer days, then the impressive **Santuário Dom Bosco,** a church with tall pointed-arch windows composed of small squares of heavenly blue glass.

most beautiful or original symbol.

Dominating the entire ensemble, the **Congresso Nacional** (National Congress) is noted for the counterpoint of its dome and inverted dome —the only visible parts of the subterranean chambers of the House of Representatives and the Federal Senate. Between these halls rise twin 28-storey administrative towers. The zoning laws assure that no building in Brasília will ever be taller.

An impressive group of **sculptures** stands in the great plaza. The best-known monument is dedicated to the Candangos, the people who came here to build the new capital. And notice the serene modern version of Justice blindfolded, sitting before the Palácio da Justiça (Supreme Court). Another greatly admired sculpture is the powerful work called *The Meteor,* by Bruno Giorgi, in the lotus pool in front of the lavish **Palácio dos Arcos** (Palace of the Arches). The building, also known as Palácio do Itamaraty, is used for diplomatic receptions, so the decor and furnishings are most elegant. To visit, though, be sure to apply for permission 24 hours in advance.

Of all Brasília's palaces, the long, low **Palácio da Alvorada** (Palace of the Dawn) is the least pompous and most human. Oscar Niemeyer is said to have designed its upside-down arches in a single night; Kubitschek hailed its "lightness, grandeur, lyricism and majesty". The palace, which serves as the presidential residence, is on the shore of a man-made lake with a perimeter of 50 miles (80 km.), called Lago Paranoá. It brightens the scenery and gives the landlocked Brasilienses a welcome chance to do some boating and fishing.

Also overlooking the lake are **Embassy Sectors North and South** (SEN and SES). Here architects from various countries tried to express the very best in national traditions or trends.

To put Brasília into perspective, take the elevator to the observation level of the **Television Tower** *(Torre de TV)* and see how Brasília fits into the all-encircling plain. Here and there you'll see an excavation site with the red earth visible like a wound in what's now such a green, tidy parkland. And from very near the centre of the pilot plan, you'll be able to judge how it all grew from a simple cross on a piece of paper.

South

CURITIBA

Introduction

From the first moment, Curitiba shows you the spirit of the south. Its office and apartment blocks soar upwards in white and pastel shades, but in an unusually aesthetic way. Multistorey they may be—claustrophobic they're certainly not. Throughout the city, there's a comfortable blend of colonial and contemporary.

And everywhere, amazingly, glimpses of green. Landscaped corners, plant-decorated squares, tree-lined avenues, parks for pedestrians.

This is Curitiba's secret of success—somehow it allows you to breathe. Pollution has never been a problem for this relaxed metropolis during its 300 years, a hundred as capital of Paraná state. The discovery of gold in the rivers brought hordes of prospectors in the 17th century and cattle farming kept others there. Italian immigrants and later Germans and Slavs gave Paraná a many-sided personality.

Its pleasant climate and rich soil ensured that, if Brazil's coffee was to be the best in the world, Paraná's would be the best in Brazil.

Curitiba's setting, on a plateau of the Serra do Mar just over 3,000 feet above sea level, gives it a climate with more than a hint of southern Europe. No surprise that it acquired the nickname "City of the Smile" (Cidade do Sorriso).

Further west, towards the borders with Paraguay and Argentina, there's snow in the winter and the thermometer can sometimes dip alarmingly. But not for long.

About 60 miles east is the sea, and Curitiba's neighbour, the Atlantic port of Paranaguá. Between the two, a journey that would be daunting if it weren't so spectacular. By rail, the switchback route gives unsurpassed views of the lush *floresta araucária*—Brazil's famous forests of umbrella pines.

Brazilian cities aren't always famed for their sense of organization. But to many, Curitiba comes close to the idea of a rationally conceived town in carefully preserving so much breathing space for its inhabitants.

Organization in other matters may occasionally leave something to be desired. But if things don't work out exactly, the *Curitibanos*—true to their city's nickname—just keep on smiling.

A Brief History

16th-17th century	The state of Paraná begins as part of the hereditary captaincies *(capitanias hereditárias)* of São Vicente and Santana. Drawn by discoveries of gold in the rivers, settlers move into the area. Cattle farming develops. The village of Paranaguá is founded in 1653 and Curitiba follows in 1693.
18th century	The population of both the south-eastern coastal strip and the interior increases and further settlements are established, among them Guaratuba (1771), Antonina (1797) and Castro (1798).
19th century	In 1853 Paraná is separated from São Paulo and transformed into a province. It becomes a state in 1889, taking Curitiba as its capital. Six years later, Brazil acquires the region of Las Palmas, on the south-western border of Paraná, from Argentina.
20th century	Las Palmas is absorbed into Paraná in 1916, following a dispute over jurisdiction with the neighbouring state of Santa Catarina. Paraná's *terra roxa* (red earth) helps make the state Brazil's foremost coffee producer and the port of Paranaguá becomes an important export outlet for coffee beans. The economy diversifies, with cattle farming and timber competing as dollar-earning industries.

Sightseeing

One of the most interesting of Curitiba's museums is the **Museu Paranaense**, housed in the former municipal hall on Praça Generoso Marques, which has a good selection of sculptures, paintings and weapons.

The **Cathedral**, on nearby Praça Tiradentes, was built comparatively recently, in 1894. Anyone who knows Barcelona is likely to have a feeling of *déjà vu*—Curitiba's cathedral was designed after the style of the one in the Spanish city.

Curitiba manages to combine comfortably past and present in its city structures. Behind the cathedral is one of the pedestrian precincts, where you can find colonial-era buildings and a flower clock, close to the Museum of Sacred Art.

Paintings and other art exhibits go on show—and on sale—weekly on Praça Garibaldi, next to the Church of the Rosary (Igreja do Rosário), and on Praça Rui Barbosa.

A popular spot for families is the **Passeio Público**, a public park complete with a lake in the centre of town. Small boats enable you to reach the islands in the middle. The park also has a zoo and an aquarium containing a wide variety of tropical fish.

Excursions

Dizzying views are in store if you take the famous journey by rail 93 kilometres (58 mi) east to **Paranaguá**—unarguably the most unforgettable train trip anywhere in Brazil.

The three-and-a-half-hour mountain journey provides helter-skelter turns high above sheer precipices, and equally exhilarating valley panoramas as you emerge suddenly into the sunlight from one of the many tunnels. Don't miss the rushing **waterfall** close to Banhado, colourfully christened the Bride's Veil (Véu de Noiva).

Down at sea level, Paranaguá is one of the country's primary collection points for coffee. The port itself is some 29 kilometres (18 mi) from the open sea on a lagoon reachable from the Bay of Paranaguá.

While there, you can visit the waterfront **market**—where stallkeepers and merchandise reflect the mood of the south—or take a boat trip to some of the many islands in the bay. On one, about an hour out, is the fort of Nossa Senhora dos Prazeres, constructed in 1767.

Paranaguá's **Museum of Archaeology and Art** is housed in what used to be a Jesuit school, Colégio dos Jesuítas. Also worth visiting are the St. Benedict Church (Igreja de São Benedito) and the shrine of Our Lady of Rocio.

The gigantic and bizarre rock formations of **Vila Velha State Park**, 95 kilometres (60 mi.) north-west of Curitiba, make an unusual excursion. The towering sandstone shapes—some of them like animals—have been created over the centuries by continual rain and wind erosion. Near the Lagoa Dourada (Golden Lagoon) is another oddity of nature—two deep **water holes** (furnas), one with a lift, that connect with an underground lake.

South

IGUAÇU FALLS

Introduction

A whole ocean of white water comes tumbling over the lip of the world, plunging down cliffs of tropical greenery and sending up clouds of rainbow spray from the thunderous abyss below. Higher than Niagara, wider than Victoria, Iguaçu can justly claim to be the world's most impressive falls.

It is here that the Iguaçu River, racing down from the Brazilian highlands, drops sheer over the edge of the Paraná plateau into a narrow gorge. Just before the river reaches the brink, it broadens out to 2½ miles (4 km.), then cascades in a wide arc over the precipice in a series of more than 200 spectacular falls, separated by jutting rocks and islands of luxuriant vegetation.

Brazil lies on one side, Argentina on the other. To the Brazilians the falls are known (in Portuguese) as *Saltos do Iguaçu;* to the Argentines (in Spanish) as *Cataratas del Iguazú.* But the name comes originally from the local Guaraní Indian name meaning "Great Water", and however you write it, the pronunciation is Iguassu.

You should try to visit the falls from both sides: the views are magnificently different and equally awe-inspiring. On the Brazilian bank you face the whole panorama of the falls, from the cataract of Santa Maria round to the foaming Devil's Throat and on to the graceful Two Sisters, cascading down in twin torrents over ledges of green basalt rock. On the Argentine side you can venture out to islands in the swirling current below the cataracts or penetrate along catwalks above and behind white curtains of water.

But be warned: although the canyon that divides the two countries is less than 300 feet (80 m.) wide, it takes a roundabout journey of 37 miles (60 km.) by road and ferry to get from one side to the other!

Some 12 miles (20 km.) below the cataracts, the Iguaçu runs into the Paraná River on the borders of yet a third country, Paraguay; upstream on the Paraná, the world's largest hydroelectric project is under construction at Itaipu and is well worth a visit.

The Iguaçu Falls are enhanced by the vast expanse of dense jungle which surrounds them and which is protected as national park. In this primeval rainforest, rich in orchids, lianas and tree ferns, multicoloured birds and butterflies display their brilliance by day and the secretive jaguar still hunts by night. You can visit the park on either side.

Regular flights to the falls are available from Rio de Janeiro and São Paulo in Brazil, from Buenos Aires in Argentina and from Asuncion in Paraguay. There is an international airport on the Brazilian side between Foz do Iguaçu and the falls, and another airport on the Argentine side near Puerto Iguazú.

Iguaçu is one of the great sights of South America—not to be missed. Over a million visitors come here each year. They can't fail to go away a little more inspired than when they came—and a little more humble.

A Brief History

16th century	The Portuguese first land in Brazil in 1500, while the Spaniards discover neighbouring Argentina some 20 years later. In 1541, Spanish explorer Alvar Núñez Cabeza de Vaca reaches the Iguaçu Falls and christens them Salto de Santa María. But the new title never catches on, and they revert to their original Guaraní name, leaving only the first cataract on the Brazilian side to be called Santa Maria.
18th century	Jesuit missionaries reach the falls but have to abandon their studies of them when they are expelled from South America in 1767.
19th century	The first maps are made of the Iguaçu Falls in 1892. The idea of a national park for the region is mooted in 1897 by a Brazilian army officer, Edmundo de Barros.
20th century	National parks are established on both sides of the falls, in 1934 on the Argentine side and in 1939 on the Brazilian side. After World War II, tourism flourishes and hotels and airports are established on both banks.

The Virgin and the Serpent-God

Any falls as impressive as Iguaçu are bound to have their origins cloaked in a mist of legends. One such is told by the Guaraní people.

Long ago, they say, the serpent-god of the river, son of the supreme god Tupan, used to demand each year the sacrifice of the tribe's most beautiful virgin. After a solemn ceremony of ritual and dance, she was thrown into the water to appease him.

One day, it came to be the turn of the daughter of a Guaraní chief. She was so beautiful that even the river stood still when her face was mirrored in the water. Her lover, a Guaraní warrior, tried to snatch her away in his canoe. But the serpent-god, hissing and writhing in fury, split open the earth and poured the river waters into the chasm of the Devil's Throat, smashing the frail boat.

The young lovers escaped but were doomed to be parted: for his temerity, the warrior was turned into a tree. He stands forever on the bank, stretching his arms towards his beloved, transformed into a rock in midstream.

And from the depths of the Devil's Throat the angry rumblings of the serpent-god still echo down the canyon.

Visiting the Falls

The first sight of the falls from the Brazilian side is stupendous. From the road in front of the Hotel das Cataratas you can see the whole sweep of the cataracts, thundering down a giant staircase of rock between islands of green. There are altogether 275 falls and the 20 main ones all have names.

Nearest to the Brazilian side are **Floriano** and **Deodoro**, dropping onto a green ledge halfway down before plunging over the **Santa Maria** cataract into the gorge below. Beyond them you will see the falls of **Benjamin Constant** and **União**, before the terrifying **Devil's Throat** *(Garganta do Diabo)* spews out a cloud of spray from the innermost corner of the falls, where the Brazilian and Argentine frontiers meet.

Beyond the Devil's Throat on the Argentine flank, the white wall of water that seems to rush straight out of the jungle is known as the **Mitré**. Then come **Rivadavia** and the **Three Musketeers,** foaming round the island of San Martin, where the trees are almost submerged in flood season. The perpetual spray creates a miniature tropical rainforest on the islands in the very heart of the falls.

Further round again are the slender **Adam and Eve** falls, **Two Sisters** *(Dos Hermanas)* and the last big fall, **Cabeza de Vaca,** which honours the Spaniard who first saw Iguaçu.

The luxury government-owned **Hotel das Cataratas** which commands this panorama is a vast colonial-style building, complete with garden and open-air swimming-pool.

A **heliport** provides helicopter flights over the falls. The best way to get a close-up view, however, is on foot. A two-hour round trip will take you down steps, through a forested path and along spectacular **catwalks** swept by spray (take a raincoat) to the very edge of the falls on the Brazilian side and to an observation tower. Small boats with

A cloud of spray cloaks the mighty waters of Iguaçu.

outboard motors will also take you out on the river from **Porto Canoa** above the falls.

The joint Brazilian-Paraguayan dam project at **Itaipu** up the Paraná river provides an interesting day's excursion by car or boat. If you go by boat, watch for the marker in the water at the junction of the Iguaçu and Paraná rivers which denotes the meeting point of the three countries, Brazil, Argentina and Paraguay.

At Itaipu, the waters of the Paraná have been diverted through a giant canal on the Brazilian side, and the plant, which will be the world's biggest hydroelectric enterprise, is already in operation. Waters backing up to form a 320,000-acre (130,000-ha.) lake will eventually drown the spectacular Guaíra Falls, higher up on the Paraná, hitherto the world's greatest falls in volume of water. (They are known as Sete Quedas, or Seven Falls, to the Brazilians.)

When all 20 turbines are working, Itaipu will have a generating capacity of 12.6 million kilowatts—enough to supply one-third of Brazil's needs and more than the combined capacity of the Aswan dam in Egypt and the Grand Coulee in the U.S.

A Jungle for Jaguars

The Iguaçu Falls and the jungle area all around them are strictly protected. Brazil and Argentina have established contiguous national parks which together cover more than 494,000 acres (200,000 ha.). Both have an extensive network of trails as well as visitor centres to explain the natural history of the forest and the falls. Take binoculars if you go into the forest.

The vegetation is remarkable in its variety, ranging from pines to coconut palms, giant tree ferns, bamboos and begonias. Epiphytes, including numerous kinds of orchid, flourish in the moist atmosphere. Birds are conspicuous, including toucans, parrots and herons.

Mammals are less visible, but you may like to know that the forest shelters such species as the jaguar, puma, ocelot, tapir and giant anteater, as well as some rare species of monkey. In the evening, iridescent butterflies hover above the falls, and caymans (a kind of alligator) come out to bask on the rocks.

Though hunting is banned, fishing is allowed within the parks. Fish include *dourado* (golden salmon), *mandi, cascudo* and various kinds of catfish.

South

PORTO ALEGRE

Introduction

Strategically placed at the meeting-point of five rivers, Porto Alegre—capital of Rio Grande do Sul—is Brazil's southernmost metropolis. On the one side, a dynamic fresh-water port that ships out beef, tobacco, rice, wool and cereals as fast as the state can produce them. On the other, the start of the pampas—vast grassy plains that stretch across into Uruguay and Argentina, home of the South American gaucho.

For almost two centuries after the discovery of Brazil, this region was the domain of the Spanish. Later, the Portuguese arrived, adding to the already cosmopolitan mixture of Iberian influence and Indian heritage. Then came the Italians... followed by the Germans. Today's *gaúcho* has an understandably col-ourful air, with his plus-four pants, widebrimmed hat, ban-dana, knife, ornamental belt and famous leather boots that go up or down like a concer-tina.

Here, you can feast on *chur-rasco,* huge chunks of prime beef grilled over hot coals. To wash it down—*erva-mate,* green herbal tea, or a bottle of "Italian" wine from the vine-yards of the south.

There are plenty of beaches. The River Guaíba runs into an immense lagoon, the Lagoa dos Patos (Lagoon of the Ducks), which discharges roughly half as much water into the sea as the Amazon. Coming in as that goes out are a succession of cargo ships that make Porto Alegre the most important trading port in southern Brazil.

Softening any harsh out-lines: the spectacular sunsets of the south that bring a re-splendent glow to the evening sky over the Guaíba.

A Brief History

18th century	Portuguese interest in the Spanish settlement of Colonia del Sacramento prompts them in 1737 to found Rio Grande, in the far south. Three years later, settlers from Açores and Laguna arrive as part of a planned pro-gramme of colonization. Porto dos Casais—subse-quently renamed Porto Alegre—comes into being. The century is marked by clashes along the border between Portuguese and Spanish settlers.

19th century	Rio Grande captaincy becomes autonomous in 1807. A year later Porto Alegre receives town status. With the declaration of Brazilian independence in 1822, Rio Grande is redefined as the province of Rio Grande do Sul. The first immigrants of German origin arrive in 1824.
	A militant anti-monarchist movement is formed in the south in 1835. During the next ten years, battles rage against imperial forces. The civil conflict becomes known as the War of the Rags (Guerra dos Farrapos), so called because of the battle attire of the rebel forces.
	In 1875, Italian settlers move into the province and wine is produced for export. Fourteen years later, in 1889, Rio Grande do Sul is made into a state.
20th century	In 1930, the former Governor of Porto Alegre, Getúlio Vargas, unsuccessfully contests national presidential elections but—helped by military intervention—becomes President of Brazil.

Sightseeing

Despite the huge encroaching office and business blocks, Porto Alegre's old town retains fragments of colonial charm. The **Governor's Palace** (Palácio do Governador), on Praça Marechal Deodoro, is still imposing if somewhat subdued by its 20th-century counterpart, the building of the legislative assembly (Assembléia Legislativa). Look for the twin towers of the **Igreja de Nossa Senhora das Dores** and the modern stone **cathedral,** similarly subdued.

You can stroll for a while along the pedestrianized **Rua da Praia,** Porto Alegre's hub.

By early evening, the crowds thronging the streets, bars and cafés will help give the distinct impression that you're seeing the world pass by.

Nowhere is the personality of southern Brazil more in evidence than at the **Public Market** (Mercado Público), beside the Prefeitura (Town Hall). Spot the similarity with the Mercado da Figueira in the Portuguese capital, Lisbon.

The **Parque Farroupilha** —one of Brazil's biggest parks —takes its name from the *Farrapos,* the anti-monarchist forces of last century. Set in 30 hectares (74 acres) of land, the park has ornamental gardens and a Chinese Corner (Recanto Chinês) which contains a pagoda and boating lake.

Porto Alegre's most important museum, the **Museu Júlio de Castilhos,** was set up by the state in 1903 to conduct anthropological studies of the first inhabitants and examine the area's natural history. The museum's historical documents and items of Jesuit art make a visit worthwhile.

Sailing is popular, and boat excursions can be made to islands of the 3-mile-wide River Guaíba, spanned at one point by a bridge 15 kilometres (9 mi.) long. A string of beaches line the river.

Excursions

Atlantic coast beaches can be reached effortlessly via Osório, which is linked to Porto Alegre by a smooth asphalt road. Not far on, **Tramandaí**—130 kilometres (81 mi.) from Porto Alegre—is a more sophisticated resort. From here, it's only a short distance through Capão da Canoa and Atlântida to **Torres** (Towers). Here, a series of cozy beaches nestle at the foot of towering basalt cliffs.

A pleasant mountain drive takes you to **Caxias do Sul,** 122 kilometres (76 mi.) north of Porto Alegre. This is the heart of the grape-growing region, and has strong Italian associations. At 750 metres (2,461 ft.) above sea level, Caxias has a European climate and occasional winter snow to go with it. The town's famous Grape Festival, the Festa da Uva, is as animated as any carnival.

A few miles south-east, in the undulating Serra Gaúcha, a change of atmosphere greets you, this time Germanic. The towns of **Gramado** (Grassy Area) and **Canela** (Cinnamon) have Bavarian-style houses adorned with hydrangea, a lingering fragrance of wild flowers in spring and endless opportunities for walking on the wooded hillsides and valleys.

One sight worth seeing is the **Caracol State Park** in Canela, which has a particularly dramatic waterfall, the Cascata do Caracol, that tumbles down from a height of 300 ft. over a cavernous break in the rock face.

About 37 kilometres (23 mi.) further on is the Aparados da Serra National Park and a fantastic quirk of nature —the gigantic **Itaimbezinho Canyon.** Early-morning visibility is needed to best appreciate the breathtaking vista. The split in the earth's surface extends for several miles.

Other Cities at a Glance

Florianópolis (South)

Two bridges—one the longest suspension bridge of steel in Brazil—link the southern state of Santa Catarina with its "island" capital. Prettily-decorated houses give glimpses of the Portuguese colonial past, an impression strengthened by the two forts—São José da Ponta Grossa and Santana, with its military museum. Another historically interesting building is the 18th-century church of Nossa Senhora da Conceição.

Picturesque bays around the island reveal dozens of soft-sand beaches, all easily accessible by bus. To the north of Florianópolis is the slumbering Itajaí Valley, an appropriate setting for Blumenau and other towns founded in the last century by German settlers, for many of whom the valley provided nostalgic memories of the Rhine.

Goiânia (Centre-West)

This expansive city—capital of Goiás state—is another startling example of Brazil's 20th-century planning. Tree-lined avenues give a sense of airy proportion to the modern façades. Built in 1933, 203 kilometres (126 miles) from what was to be the site of Brasília, Goiânia now has more than 700,000 inhabitants, many of them agricultural workers.

Tourists head for the Mutuama Park educational centre and the zoological gardens. Goiânia is also a sport-conscious city. Being more than six hundred miles from the Atlantic is no problem—you can water-ski comfortably in a giant reservoir.

Aracaju (North-east)

A relaxed air on—and off—the warm-water beaches belies the status of this neat, unassuming little city. But Aracaju, tucked into the bank of the River Sergipe, does have the honour of being administrative centre of Sergipe state ... albeit the smallest. Stroll along the criss-cross streets to the city park, resplendent in tropical green. Local artisans have a talent for wood carving, leatherwork and ceramics, and the fruits of their labours can be seen in the handicraft centre.

Not far south-west of town is the former capital, São Cristóvão. Beautifully-preserved churches include the Igreja de Nossa Senhora da Misericórdia (Our Lady of Mercy), built early in the 17th century, together with the later convents of São Francisco (1693) and Carmo (1766).

Maceió (North-east)

An architectural delight awaits you, with the dreamlike quality of Maceió's neatly-tiled homes and public buildings. Particularly picturesque are the tile-covered church of Bom Jesus dos Mártires and the Government Palace. The city—capital of Alagoas state and a busy sugar port—also has another claim to fame: an exotic local dish prepared from *sururu*, a shellfish found in the nearby lagoon.

The beaches—Jatiúca, Jacarecica, Guacuma and Garcia Torte—are as exotic as they sound. Many local people will say they are the best in Brazil. You can get to them within half an hour.

João Pessoa (North-east)

Majestic coconut palms line the glistening sands of Brazil's easternmost mainland point, where the Paraíba River flows out from the state of the same name into the Atlantic. Architecture ranges from the baroque to the super-future: the 18th-century church of São Francisco shares room with a huge circular hotel poised on the edge of the sea like an inverted flying saucer.

João Pessoa's monasteries are worth a visit, and the tropical parks offer a few quiet moments in this otherwise animated state capital of 300,000 people. The farthest point east (not counting the Brazilian islands) is marked by the lighthouse of Ponta do Seixas.

Natal (North-east)

Jungle gradually gives way to the golden sand dunes of Natal and the curious star-shaped fort around which a settlement began to take shape back in 1599. Today, almost 400 years later, waves still lap serenely around the stone Forte dos Reis Magos, but the rest of the once-tiny settlement has moved with the times: Natal—population a quarter of a million—has become capital of Rio Grande do Norte state and focal point of the country's space research programme.

The placid waters around the fort are teeming with marine life that is fascinating to see. And the city has fine freshwater beaches as well as the coastal ones.

São Luís (North-east)

Delightful ornamental buildings from the early 17th century are everywhere to be seen in São Luís, founded as a port in 1612 by French settlers. Steep streets lead to some of the oldest mansions of colonial times, occupied first by the French, then the Dutch, and finally the Portuguese. São Luís—Maranhão state capital—is set between two bays on an island which gave the city its name and an enviable setting.

The finest churches include Santana, Carmo and Rosário. These, together with Ribeirão fort and the ruins of the fort of São Sebastião, help trace the outline of the city's many-faceted history.

OTHER CITIES

Eating Out

In the melting pot of Brazil, three quite different concepts of a square meal interacted delectably over the centuries. The Indians first contributed grains, vegetables and seafood, the Portuguese brought their stews, and African slaves added new spices and sauces. Stir in ethnic influences from Spain, France, Poland, China, Japan, Germany and Italy, and you have a fascinating array of culinary possibilities.

Brazil is today one of the world's top cattle-producing countries, so the meat is first-class. The South Atlantic provides a bonanza of fish and seafood. In the tropics, familiar fruits and vegetables are juicier than ever, and unfamiliar ones excite the palate.

Fish and Seafood

Many city people will have their lunches at *lanchonetes* —stand-up snack bars where you can meet the locals and try some Brazilian appetizers: deep fried shrimp and bean patties, fish balls and *salgados* (savoury pies).

Fresh fish fillets are boiled, blended, roasted or marinated in mouth-watering combinations with crisp vegetables and tropical fruit. They are liberally seasoned with spices such as coriander, pepper and *urucum* (a fruit which gives a red colour), then soaked in fresh lime and lemon juice.

Filé de peixe (fish fillet) often turns out to be *badejo* (bass). You can also get excellent sole *(linguado)*. Reasonably priced seafood dishes include *zarzuela de mariscos,* a thick Spanish version of a *bouillabaisse.*

The Brazilians have added spice to Portugal's fish chowders, notably *caldeirada* or *frutos do mar ensopados* and *bacalhau,* dried salt cod baked in a rich sauce.

Moqueca capixaba is a fish stew with onions, garlic, tomatoes and spices, served with onion gravy and *pirão,* a flour porridge made with fish stock. *Muma de siri* is a kind of porridge with small crabs, onions and tomatoes, served with rice. *Torta capixaba,* a seafood pie consisting of lobster, crab, oysters, shrimps, fresh fish, onion, hearts of palm, tomatoes and spices, is served with rice and fried manioc flour. Shark is another speciality, with some regional adaptations such as *cação do lameirão à vitória* in Vitória.

Brazil's foremost contributions to the art of cooking come from the north-east, where the Indian, African and European currents meet. Two celebrated dishes:

Vatapá. This Bahian speciality includes shrimp, fish, grated coconut, ground peanuts, cashew nuts, tomato, onion, hot pepper, ginger, coriander, olive oil and *dendê* oil, the yellowish palm oil indispensable to Bahian cooking.

Xinxim (pronounced shing-SHING), is a chicken stew cooked with ground dried shrimp, hot spices and *dendê* oil.

Acarajé is a big fritter made from a batter of ground beans, deep-fried in boiling *dendê* oil. The resultant dumpling is split down the middle and liberally filled with *vatapá* (see above), dried shrimp and hot *malagueta* pepper sauce. Served as a starter or snack.

Fish dishes are tempting in Salvador, and so is the shellfish—crab, lobster, prawns and squid. Restaurants in the port area specialize in seafood preparations like *camarões* (prawns), fried or stewed in tomato sauce and garlic, and *casquica,* a spicy crab dish. Seafood snacks are also widely sold in the street.

Fortaleza is Brazil's lobster capital and one of the world's leading producers of spiny lobsters or crayfish. The place to eat it is at one of the restaurants on Futuro beach, where much of the lobster catch comes in. Most restaurants will make *lagosta* their speciality and serve it in one form or another.

(Lobster is too expensive to be everyday food for most local people, and they will more likely sit down to simpler fare—*baião de dois,* pork with rice and beans; *bife (or frango) com arroz e feijão,* steak or chicken with rice and black beans; or *canja,* a chicken, ham and rice soup.)

Seafood specialities include *bobó,* prawns cooked in a sauce of sweet cassava, coconut milk and tomatoes; and *caruru,* prawns with okra and peanuts.

Tasty fish from the Amazon includes *tambaqui, tucanaré* and the huge *pirarucu.* If you decide to order this, don't ask for a whole one unless you have an appetite to match it—the pirarucu is up to 6 feet long and can weigh over 200 pounds. There are also many

The best of Brazilian cuisine served with an irresistible smile.

varieties of catfish, mostly good eating.

Another popular dish in the Amazon region is *tacacá* —dried shrimps prepared with a mixture of *tucupi* and *jambu,* a herb reputed locally to have aphrodisiac powers. If you're disappointed, you can always drown your sorrows without suffering too many after-effects—*tucupi* is said to be an excellent remedy for hangovers!

Down in south-western Brazil, the Iguaçu and Paraná rivers yield excellent fish, especially the golden salmon *(dourado)*. While there, you should try the palm-heart salads, which are particularly delicious. Most hotels also serve appetizing buffets of a variety of Brazilian and international foods.

Meat Dishes

Brazil is the land of the large appetite and you'll need one to enjoy the national dish, *feijoada completa*. Based on a variety of salted and smoked meats cooked with spices, vegetables and beans, it is served with toasted cassava flour and egg, shredded kale and or-

Grilled to order, a churrasco steak is a feast to remember.

anges for a hint of sweetness.

The state of Minas Gerais, north of Rio, provides an exquisite alternative—*tutu,* a subtle mixture of black beans, bacon, sausage or jerked beef, manioc meal and onion, usually served with shredded kale and hard-boiled egg.

In the south, beef comes into its own. Gaucho-style barbecues at *churrascarias* offer mouth-watering steaks or chops, skewered and grilled over charcoal. If you seriously think your appetite can defeat the supply, ask for *rodízio,* which means there's a fixed price for as much as you can eat. Chicken grills are a slightly less filling alternative.

As the main outlet for the Amazon produce, Belém is the natural place to sample regional dishes. One of the most famous is *pato no tucupi,* duck served in a tingling aromatic sauce made from manioc juice mixed with peppers.

Maniçoba is best eaten at a good restaurant; some of the ingredients can take up to a week to prepare. They include *maniva* (manioc leaf), sausage, *mocotó* (beef marrow), ham and *jaba* (sun-dried meat).

However hot it is, there's a fruit to quench any thirst.

Turtle has long been a delicacy, but it's served rarely now, in an effort to protect the animal. The flesh can be prepared in 17 different ways.

Desserts

If you have problems deciding on the main course, the choice of dessert will be even harder. Throughout Brazil, there are about a hundred different flavours to choose from—fresh fruit or nuts or any combination imaginable in the form of a sorbet. The widest range is usually found in the Amazon area.

The Brazilians from the north-east, surrounded as they are by sugar cane, have developed a sweet tooth and a number of satisfying puddings. Try *pudim de abóbora*, pumpkin pudding, or *creme de abacate*, chilled cream of avocado. A traditional sweet from the sugar plantations is *quindins de Iaiá*, coconut cup cakes.

Drinks

Brazil's most popular aperitif, the *caipirinha*, is similar to a Mexican margarita, but the firewater is *cachaça*, distilled from sugar cane. A *batida* is a cocktail, whipped up in a blender, of *cachaça*, ice, sugar and fruit juice.

Drink it neat, and you'll soon understand why it's also known as *aguardente*—"burning water"!

There are locally made gins, whiskies and vermouths, but local beers are particularly good: ask for an ice-cold *chope*. Brazilian wine, from the far south of the country, is well worth sampling, as is the refreshing southern herbal tea, *erva-mate*.

Sucos, fruit drinks, come in a variety of extraordinary fla-

The moment every sunbather waits for . . . ice-cold mate.

vours, including cashew, passion fruit, papaya and guava.

Cool yourself with a *vinho de açaí,* made from the pap of a kind of palm and manioc flour, or one of the other mouthwatering concoctions: *guaraná, bacaba* (also palm fruits), or *cupuaçu, pariri, tucumã, murici* . . . the names are as exotic as the tastes. A sip of any one, or some ice-cold *mate,* is a delicious way to wash the salt off your lips after a swim.

And then, of course, there's the renowned Brazilian coffee. What better way to round off your meal than with a traditional *cafezinho,* a demitasse of coffee extract as sweet as it's strong.

Brazilians like it very sweet and very often. If you don't want too much sugar, protest in good time.

To Help You Order...

Could we have a table? **Queríamos uma mesa.**

I'd like a/an/some... **Queria...**

beer	**uma cerveja**	milk	**leite**
bill	**a conta**	mineral water	**uma água mineral**
bread	**pão**	napkin	**um guardanapo**
butter	**manteiga**	potatoes	**batatas**
coffee	**um café**	rice	**arroz**
dessert	**sobremesa**	salad	**uma salada**
fish	**peixe**	sandwich	**um sanduíche**
fruit	**fruta**	soup	**sopa**
ice cream	**um sorvete**	sugar	**açúcar**
meat	**carne**	tea	**chá**
menu	**o cardápio**	wine	**vinho**

...and Read the Menu

abacaxi	pineapple	**framboesas**	raspberries
alho	garlic	**frango**	chicken
almôndegas	meatballs	**frito**	fried
arroz	rice	**goiaba**	guava
assado	roasted	**grelhado**	grilled
azeitonas	olives	**lagosta**	spiny lobster
bacalhau	cod	**laranja**	orange
badejo	sea bass	**legumes**	vegetables
bife	beefsteak	**limão**	lemon
bolo	cake	**maçã**	apple
cabrito	kid	**melancia**	watermelon
camarão	shrimp	**morangos**	strawberries
caranguejo	crab	**ovo**	egg
carneiro	lamb	**peixe**	fish
cavala	mackerel	**pescadinha**	whiting
chouriço	a spicy sausage	**pimentão**	green pepper
costeletas	pork ribs	**queijo**	cheese
dobrada	tripe	**siri**	beach crab
enguias	eel	**sobremesa**	dessert
feijão	beans	**sorvete**	ice cream
fígado	liver	**uva**	grapes
flan	caramel custard	**vitela**	veal

Shopping

Rio's most sophisticated boutiques are in Ipanema. Copacabana has more variety, except for clothing, and prices are normally a bit lower. A third good bet is the pedestrian area in the business centre or Botafogo's Rio-Sul shopping centre.

There are several shopping centres spaced out along São Paulo's broad *avenidas*, such as the huge Ibirapuera project.

You'll find plenty of chic boutiques (especially in the Avenida Paulista and Rua Augusta), jewellers, arts and crafts and souvenir shops.

Shopping in Brasília is not conventional—there are eight large complexes where most goods can be bought without too much searching. The Conjunto Nacional, north side of

The art market—a treasure trove for souvenir-seekers.

the Rodoviária, is one of the biggest shopping centres in South America. Less modern is a handicraft, bric-a-brac market held at the foot of the TV Tower each Saturday and Sunday, good for a browse.

There is no doubt that **gemstones** are one of the most popular buys. Amethysts, aquamarines, opals, topazes, tourmalines, diamonds, emeralds, rubies and sapphires—all nine are mined in Brazil. Stones can be bought uncut,

Shopping, Brazilian style: the last thing you need is a roof.

cut but not set, or made into rings, pendants or bracelets.

The north-east is famous throughout Brazil for its **carved tropical hardwoods** and pottery or wooden **figurines,** often reflecting the African origins of its people. Pottery figurines have become collectors' items, the old ones being the rarest and most valuable.

Open-air markets in Olinda and Recife are ideal places to come across the unexpected. More usual are **leatherwork, Indian hammocks, butterflies, lace, soapstone carvings, ceramics** and **cigars.**

Like the women of Salvador, a Bahian **doll** wears large earrings and a lacy dress, with colourful fruit balanced in a head basket.

Silverware is also one of Salvador's specialities. But look for the hallmark, as not all pieces are genuine.

Jewellery of many kinds is on sale. The *penca de balangandãs* is a sort of pendant-brooch dating back to slave days. On it are attached various charms including the *figa* (the Brazilian thumb-in-fist symbol), which wards off the evil eye. Take a look, too, at the selection of necklaces, bangles and rings; it will be hard to choose.

In Fortaleza, the former jail is the shopping centre for local crafts—**ceramics, leatherwork, embroidery** and the exquisite **lace** fashioned by the women of Fortaleza while their menfolk spend long hours at sea in their *jangadas.*

Pottery **figurines** in this area are full of humour and ingenuity as well as colour.

Fortaleza's artists display

Hats to fit every head—and this head can take 50.

their **paintings** in city squares and you may find that some of the naive works are particularly good.

In the more sophisticated shops, a wide range of **precious and semi-precious stones** from the Minas Gerais area are on offer, but you will need to be an expert to compare prices and quality.

The markets have a large variety of traditional **Indian crafts** on display. Indian **hammocks** make good souvenirs, as they pack easily and are light to carry.

Not surprisingly, Indian handicraft is everywhere to be seen in Belém's souvenir shops, particularly strongly coloured **ceramic** items. Good-quality **pottery, paintings** and **hardwood carvings** can be found at the Feira do Artesanato in Praça Kennedy.

The women of Belém weave intricate **wall coverings.** They are also adept at **basketwork,** and fashion decorative **dolls** from palm leaves.

Precious stones are widely available, as well as inlaid boxes and bracelets in silver-tin.

Simpler gifts include those made from **shells** or **beads,** and **coloured sand pictures** in bottles. Local craftsmen use **bird feathers** imaginatively for decoration and pictures.

Open-air markets sell a wide variety of tropical flowers and scented plants.

Don't be tempted by anyone offering reptile skins or the furs of jaguar or other spotted cats; the trade is illegal and most countries will not allow you to import products of endangered species.

Souvenir check list:

Antiques. Colonial-era religious statuettes or ceremonial swords and painted tiles.

Batik prints of Brazilian folklore themes.

Ceramics. Jugs, bowls, stoneware vases.

Coffee. You'll never be closer to the source.

Dolls, especially in Bahia costumes with colourful hats.

Dresses. Simple, cool and comfortable in the tropical sun.

Indian products. Spears, blowpipes, tomahawks, jewellery and other items from northern Brazilian tribes.

Jacaranda wood salad bowls and trays.

Kites of cloth in fighting-bird shape and bright colours.

Lace. Patiently stitched articles of all kinds and sizes.

Leather. Bags, belts, wallets and shoes.

Musical instruments. Flutes and the wonderful percussion instruments of Carnival fame.

Plants. The miraculous *pau d'água* looks like a dead stick, but flourishes when you add water.

Recordings (discs and tapes) of sambas, bossa nova tunes and folk music.

Straw bags, baskets, hats.

Swimsuits—if they're not too daring back home.

BRAZIL
BRIEFING

ARRIVAL. Canadian, British and Irish nationals and citizens of most Commonwealth countries need only a passport to enter Brazil, while visitors from Australia, New Zealand, South Africa and the U.S. must obtain a visa. No vaccinations are required unless you are arriving from, or have recently visited, countries infected with certain serious diseases (cholera, yellow fever, etc.). In case of doubt, consult a travel agent well in advance of your departure date.

The following chart shows the duty-free items you may take into Brazil and, when returning home, into your own country:

Into:	Cigarettes		Cigars		Tobacco	Spirits		Wine
Brazil	400	and	25	and	250 g.	2 l.		
Australia	200	or	250 g.	or	250 g.	1 l.	or	1 l.
Canada	200	and	50	and	900 g.	1.1 l.	or	1.1 l.
Eire	200	or	50	or	250 g.	1 l.	and	2 l.
N. Zealand	200	or	50	or	250 g.	1.1 l.	and	4.5 l.
S. Africa	400	and	50	and	250 g.	1 l.	and	2 l.
U.K.	200	or	50	or	250 g.	1 l.	and	2 l.
U.S.A.	200	and	100	and	*	1 l.	or	1 l.
* a reasonable quantity								

BANKS and CURRENCY EXCHANGE. Banking hours are normally from 10 a.m. to 4.30 p.m. weekdays, although you may find that currency can be changed only up to 12 or 1 o'clock. Banks at international airports are open later. Authorized banks change foreign currency and traveller's cheques into cruzados at the official exchange rate. Don't change too much at a time, and be sure to keep receipts as you're allowed to resell only 30% of the cruzados you have legally bought. Make sure you have your passport with you.

Another way to change money is on the charmingly named "parallel market", which does not give receipts. The exchange rate tends to be more favourable (around 20%) than the bank rate, but you have to shop around—and it's at your own risk. Your hotel porter may know where to direct you. Alternatively, look for one of the travel agencies with a *Câmbio* (exchange) sign in the window.

CAR HIRE. International and local car-hire agencies have offices at the airports, in the business centres of major cities and in other tourist areas. Their fleets range from Volkswagen "beetles" to large air-conditioned sedans. Some companies will hire cars only to drivers over 25 who have held a licence for at least one year. Normally, third-party insurance is included in the charge, but collision insurance is a sizeable extra. A federal tax of 5% is added to the bill.

Once you have a car, the only other thing you need is strong nerves. Drivers in cities like Rio, São Paulo and Belo Horizonte are not all noted for their courtesy, nor are they fanatical about obeying signals and laws. Even bus drivers sometimes ignore red lights—especially late at night—if they're in a hurry and no other traffic is visible. Pedestrians should be extremely cautious, for they have the lowest priority in the scheme of things. The laws, insofar as they are observed, follow normal international practice. Maximum speed is 80 kilometres per hour (50 mph), with a 50-kph (30-mph) limit in towns.

Always make sure that there's a service station somewhere between you and an empty fuel tank and, if so, that it will still be open when you get there. Generally, service stations close from about 8 p.m. during the week and at certain times over the weekend may be open only for the sale of diesel or alcohol-based fuel.

CLOTHING. One thing you don't need is a fur coat, but if you travel around extensively take something for all other weathers—ideally, light cotton wear supplemented by sweater and umbrella for changes of climate. The umbrella is particularly useful in the north, where equatorial temperatures and almost-daily showers keep things hot but humid. Wear a hat and long-sleeved shirt. For women, trousers (and no perfume) are recommended, to avoid attracting mosquitoes. Along Brazil's eastern coast, humidity is also high. It's drier inland and cooler in high-altitude areas, despite the tropical sun. The south is renowned for its southern-European-style climate—but, sub-tropical or not, that can mean a flurry of snow in an otherwise mild winter.

The relaxed informality may surprise travellers from conservative countries where swimwear, or even shorts, would be unthinkable in a restaurant or store. Even in the business district of Rio, among bankers and executives sweltering in suits and ties, a tourist in shorts goes unremarked. Apart from a few businessmen's restaurants off the usual tourist beat, head waiters don't worry about formality. But too-casual or shirtless patrons are barred from some restaurants. Shorts are not allowed on inter-city buses. A certain degree of modesty is called for when visiting churches or government offices.

CREDIT CARDS and TRAVELLER'S CHEQUES. Most hotels, restaurants, stores and car-hire agencies accept the major credit cards. It is certainly safer to hold your holiday funds in traveller's cheques, which can be reclaimed if lost, rather than in cash. Whenever you cash a cheque, it's a good idea to make a note of it.

CRIME and THEFT. Crime is a very real problem in Brazil. Always keep any valuables in the hotel safe. Take nothing of value to the beaches, where "beach rats" are adept at stealing the belongings of careless or unwary tourists. Beware of pickpockets in crowds and on buses. Stay clear of lonely beaches and unlit streets, and avoid displaying elegant clothing, or jewellery—real or imitation.

CURRENCY. The *cruzado* (Cz $) is divided into 100 *centavos*. However, some old banknotes in cruzeiros are still in use. Cr$1,000 = Cz$1. Coins: 50 centavos, Cz$ 1, 5, 10 and 50. Notes: Cr$ 5,000, 10,000, 50,000 and 100,000; Cz$ 10, 50, 100, 500, 1,000 and 5,000
   Note: Brazil changes its currency with depressing regularity. To further confuse the tourist, the New Cruzado (introduced in 1988) equals 1,000 cruzados.

ELECTRIC CURRENT *(corrente elétrica)*. In most places, the current is 110-volt, 60 cycles—the same as in the United States. However, some hotels have 220-volt outlets, which are usually marked.

EMERGENCIES. If you have a serious problem, you can phone your embassy *(embaixada)* or the nearest consulate *(consulado)*. Hotel staff can often help put you in touch with the necessary Brazilian authority.

HEALTH and MEDICAL CARE. Medical insurance to cover the risk of illness or accident while in Brazil is an investment you should consider. Since the risk of malaria exists in the north, you should check with your doctor before leaving home for his recommendations on malaria prevention. Don't drink tap water and take care that an overdose of sun on the first few days doesn't spoil the rest of your stay. It's also wise to go easy on food and drink until you get over any jet lag. Hotels usually have the names of doctors who speak English, or French, German or Spanish. Your consulate should have a list, too.

Drogarias sell, among other things, many familiar patent medicines, but only *farmácias* are allowed to make up prescriptions and give injections. Your hotel or any taxi driver will know the location of any *farmácia* near you that is open outside normal hours.

LANGUAGE. Don't forget that the language of Brazil is Portuguese, not Spanish. If you say *gracias* instead of *obrigado* to a Carioca, it's a little like saying "thanks" instead of *merci* in Quebec; in effect, you're announcing that you're lumping everybody in South America into the same bag and don't care about local sensibilities—which is no way to make friends.

Though Brazilian Portuguese is easier to understand than the language of Portugal, most foreigners still find it extremely difficult. Your high-school Spanish will help you understand signs and menus, and when necessary will probably be understood. The most widely spoken foreign language is English. Well-educated people are often fluent in French or German, as well.

The Berlitz phrase book PORTUGUESE FOR TRAVELLERS covers most of the situations you're likely to encounter during a visit to Brazil, as it also gives the Brazilian expressions wherever they differ from the Portuguese of Portugal. Also useful is the Portuguese-English/English-Portuguese pocket dictionary, containing a special menu-reader supplement.

MEETING PEOPLE. The Brazilians are relaxed, friendly people who are easy to get to know. Since they are as keen on getting suntanned as any tourist, the beach is the logical place to make new friends. Some outdoor cafés also have an atmosphere conducive to meeting people. In northern and southern areas, people may sometimes appear more reserved. A word or two in Portuguese can go a long way.

NEWSPAPERS and MAGAZINES *(jornal; revista).* An English-language paper, the *Latin America Daily Post,* published in Rio, covers world and regional news. Its daily supplement, the *Brazil Herald,* contains local news, social notes, cinemas and the theatre. Entertainment listings are also found in the Portuguese-language dailies such as *O Globo* and *Jornal do Brasil.* For comprehensive world news coverage in English, the *International Herald-Tribune* is on sale in certain hotels and at newsstands. *Time* and *Newsweek* are sold every week in many cities. Book stores and selected newsstands sell many other American, British and European magazines, as well.

POST OFFICES. Look for the yellow sign "ECT"—Empresa Brasileira de Correios e Telégrafos. Branch offices tend to work from 8 a.m. to 6 p.m. (sometimes 8 p.m.) on weekdays. Post offices at international airports stay open later. If you don't know ahead of time where you'll be staying, you can have mail addressed to you *Posta Restante* and pick it up at the appropriate post office. Post offices accept telegrams, and the larger offices also have telex facilities.

Stamps can be bought at some newsstands and snack bars where you might see a yellow sign saying "Correios" and "Aqui vendemos selos". Street-corner mailboxes in Brazil are yellow. Mail is collected regularly.

PUBLIC HOLIDAYS.

Jan. 1	*Dia de Confraternizaçâo Universal*	Universal Brotherhood Day
Jan. 20	*Dia de São Sebastião*	St. Sebastian's Day (local holiday, Rio)
April 21	*Tiradentes*	Tiradentes' Day (martyr of independence)
May 1	*Dia do Trabalho*	Labour Day
Sept. 7	*Independência do Brasil*	Independence Day
Nov. 2	*Finados*	All Souls' Day
Nov. 15	*Proclamação da República*	Republic Day
Dec. 8	*Imaculada Conceição**	Immaculate Conception*
Dec. 25	*Natal*	Christmas Day
Movable dates:	*Terça-feira de Carnaval*	Shrove Tuesday
	Sexta-feira da Paixão	Good Friday
	*Corpo de Deus**	Corpus Christi*

* Religious holiday not necessarily affecting business life.

TELEPHONE. The international service, using satellites and other advanced equipment, works extremely well. Public telephones are placed in large protective domes, commonly called *orelhões* – "big ears". Orange ones are for local calls, blue ones (with "DDD" on) for long-distance. Tokens *(ficha)* are sold at most newsstands, individually or in strips. When in Rio, ask for *Local* tokens if you're ringing a local number and *DDD* tokens if the call is further afield (but you can't dial out of Brazil from a street telephone).

Hotels often let guests make local calls free but add a service charge to the tariff for international calls. At airports and other key locations, there are public telephone offices where you can make long-distance and overseas calls.

TIME DIFFERENCES. The eastern half of Brazil is on the same time year-round—GMT minus three hours. During Brazilian summer (winter in the northern hemisphere) the chart looks like this:

	L.A.	N.Y.	**Rio**	London	Sydney
January:	6 a.m.	9 a.m.	**noon**	2 p.m.	1 a.m.
July:	8 a.m.	11 a.m.	**noon**	4 p.m.	1 a.m.

It's only when you head much farther west—to Manaus, for example—that the clocks go back another hour.

TIPPING. Brazilians are not great tippers, since service is generally included. However, in top-class restaurants, a 10% tip does not go amiss, while in simpler establishments the best course is to round off the sum. The same goes essentially for taxis, and it's customary to give something to hotel porters, maids and tour guides. For the hairdresser/barber, a 10% tip is appropriate. With inflation still rampant, to avoid any embarrassment ask for advice locally.

TOILETS. Public conveniences are rare, but you can always find facilities in hotels, restaurants and bars. If there's an attendant on duty, a tip is expected. "Ladies" is *Senhoras,* "Gentlemen" *Homens.* Signs are often abbreviated "S" and "H" (you might try remembering She and He).

TOURIST INFORMATION OFFICES. For information about Brazil, contact the nearest Brazilian consulate. For tourist information once you've arrived in Brazil, you'll find that states and major cities have their own tourist set-ups. The government tourist organization, EMBRA-TUR, has its head office in Rio—Praça Maúa 7, 11th floor.

TRANSPORT. There is an extensive network of airplane and bus services throughout Brazil, far more so than with trains.

Air links. Four Brazilian airlines operate regular internal connecting flights. The Brazil Air Pass, which can only be purchased abroad, gives virtually unlimited air travel all over the country during a 21-day period.

About every half hour, from 6.30 a.m. to 10.30 p.m., there's a turbo-prop flight from Rio's Santos Dumont Airport to Congonhas Airport, near the centre of São Paulo. The airline companies pool their resources for this air bridge *(ponte aérea);* you don't need a reservation—you just get on the first plane out. Other air-bridge schemes based at Rio's international airport (Galeão), involve frequent jet flights to Brasília and Belo Horizonte.

Long-distance buses. Air-conditioned buses, some equipped as sleepers, link Rio with cities as distant as Recife and the Argentine capital, Buenos Aires. The Novo Rio bus terminal is in the Santo Cristo district of northern Rio—convenient for the drivers but not necessarily for passengers. There are frequent buses to São Paulo. If you're travelling by bus in the north, where standards of comfort and efficiency may not be as high, it's an idea to take refreshments, and sometimes a blanket, with you.

Trains. In principle, travel by train is not recommended; the journeys seem longer than by bus, prices are higher and service is both less reliable and less frequent. Luxury trains such as the sleepers between Rio and São Paulo are an exception.

Index

An asterisk (*) next to a page number indicates a map reference. Page numbers in bold type refer to main entries.

INDEX